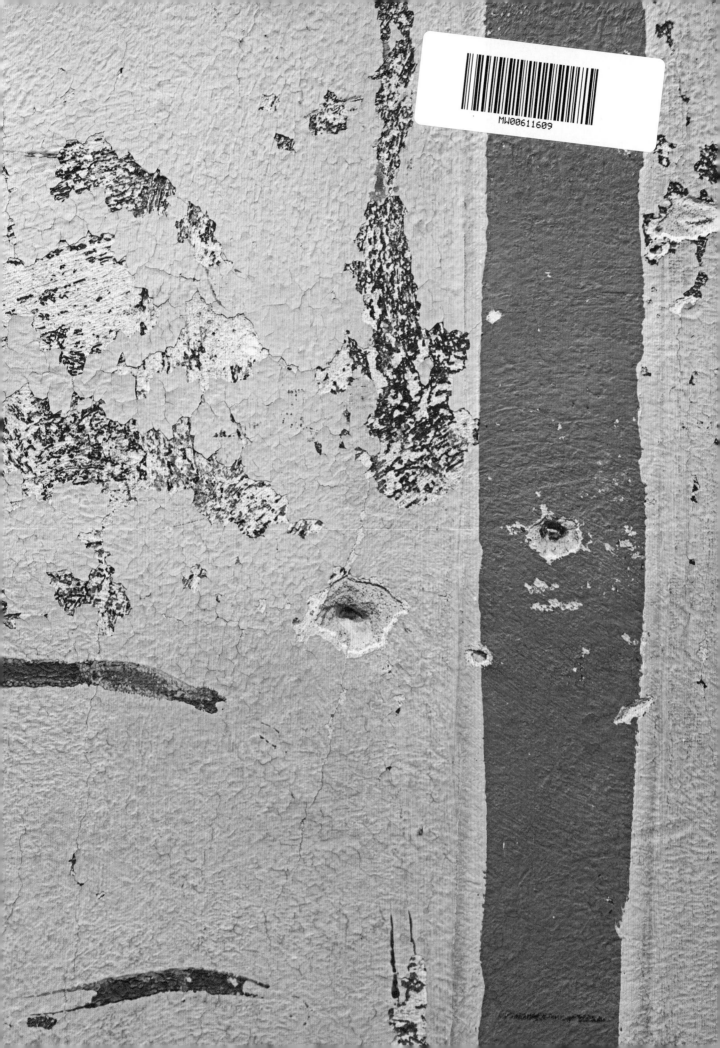

COOKING with INTUITION

BY

CARI SÁNCHEZ-POTTER
+ ROBIN RÜTENBERG

PHOTOGRAPHY BY
LAURA EVANS

For information on wholesale pricing, please e-mail beer@intuitionale.com.

ISBN: 978-0-615-88832-3

Library of Congress Cataloguing-in-Publication Data is available upon request.

Printed in the United States by Hartley Press

Book Design and Illustrations by Staci Bu Shea

INTRODUCTION

CRAFT BEERSTORY

THE INTUITION ARSENAL

PERFECT POURS

SERVING AND STORAGE

COOKING WITH INTUITION

AKNOWLEDGEMENTS

RESTAURANT INDEX

INTUITION ALE WORKS

Intuition Ale Works is a craft brewery established in 2010 in Jacksonville, Florida. We are dedicated to crafting quality, creative small batch ales. Our mission is to utilize a wide range of styles to expose and inspire our community through the vast possibilities of beer.

In February of 2012 we became the first craft brewery in the state of Florida to can our beers. We are currently canning three brands: our flagship People's Pale Ale, Jon Boat Coastal Ale and I-10 IPA. We also brew a host of draft-only, small batch specialties that can be found in our Riverside taproom.

Intuition is proud to present the creative culinary artists of Jacksonville as well as support an important community initiative, Second Harvest North Florida, through *Cooking with Intuition*. Community involvement has always been a cornerstone of Intuition Ale Works because we believe that great communities are the best environment for local businesses. A portion of the proceeds from the sale of this cookbook will go to Second Harvest North Florida.

We're very pleased to be part of one of the most thriving local communities in the South and we thank you for your support.

Ben Davis, Founder
Intuition Ale Works

SECOND HARVEST NORTH FLORIDA

Second Harvest North Florida is very proud to be partnered with Intuition Ale Works to bring you *Cooking with Intuition*. We think our partnership is a natural fit because local food and beverages are all about relationships. Second Harvest connects community organizations, corporations, local businesses and individuals to help feed the one in six adults and one in four children who are actively hungry or food insecure in north Florida. These relationships directly impact the issue of hunger in our seventeen-county service area.

On any given day, Second Harvest provides food to 350,000 individuals and just a single dollar can help distribute enough food to provide seven meals. Your purchase of this book will build a bridge between your dinner plate and that of a local person in need. We think that's a relationship we can all be proud of.

We thank you for being part of our local food community!

Bruce Ganger, Executive Director
Second Harvest North Florida

FOREWORD

In putting together this book, I've been struck by the diversity of Jacksonville's culinary talent pool. Our chefs and cooks have trained everywhere from Spain to Oregon to Miami and back again. Many of them have been honed by the lines of kitchens right here in the city or flourished under the tutelage of their own family. No matter where they learned their craft, the uniting factor is the passion they have for spreading joy through food.

Anyone who has called the First Coast home knows Jacksonville is a big city but a very, very small town. Area-wise, Jacksonville is the largest city in the continental U.S. Yet if you pick up a national food or lifestyle magazine you'll rarely see our city featured. We'd like to believe it's because we're quiet in our pride and we like to keep our treasures to ourselves. Fortunately, those attitudes are changing rapidly. Jacksonville can no longer be overlooked when discussing fine food and drink in today's South.

So why create a beer cookbook? Each of our contributing authors, whether they are food bloggers, restaurateurs, food truck chefs, philanthropists or home cooks, puts an emphasis on quality ingredients. As Intuition became part of the North Florida community, we saw the willingness by local chefs and cooks to incorporate great craft beer into their menus and dishes. Beer and food bring people together. They complement one another, some say even better than wine. We're a town filled with down-to-earth folks who love food and drink. Craft beer has become an obvious partner in that community.

One of the first things we did when we opened our tap room was create the Mug Club to foster this sense of community. Mug Club members are alloted personal mugs to claim and drink from when they visit the tap room. Special Mug Club potlucks have become a highlight of the program. One night, looking out over the many diverse and thoughtful dishes, we came to realize that we needed to share the union between craft beer and food with the world.

While creating the book you now hold in your hands, I had the privilege of talking with each one of the chefs and cooks featured within. It was a very exciting experience to hear about their dreams for the future. It's a thrilling time in Jacksonville's culinary landscape. Our food culture is coming into its own as many of our restaurants expand, our favorite chefs fire up new restaurants, food trucks bravely roll into parking lots with new food experiences and home cooks innovate for their friends and families. Our local breweries are contributing finely crafted beverages to this growing culinary repertoire and helping Jacksonville define a cultural and culinary identity.

My hope is that this cookbook is but one step in spreading the word about Jacksonville's culinary achievements, culture and dreams. There's a sense of excitement in Jacksonville, a feeling that we are collectively on the verge of something big and the contributors to this book are willing to make their dreams a reality. Thanks for joining us!

Cari Sánchez-Potter, General Manager
Intuition Ale Works

MEET THE BREWERS

Throughout this book, you'll find little quips and tips from our brewers.
They sacrifice their bodies and sanity daily to make magic happen.
Cheers to our yeast wranglers!

Ben Davis
Founder

Andrew Cattell
Head Brewer, Production Manager

Jessie O'Brien
Assistant Brewer

Matt Crossland
Assistant Brewer

Nathan Fulton
Experimental Brewer

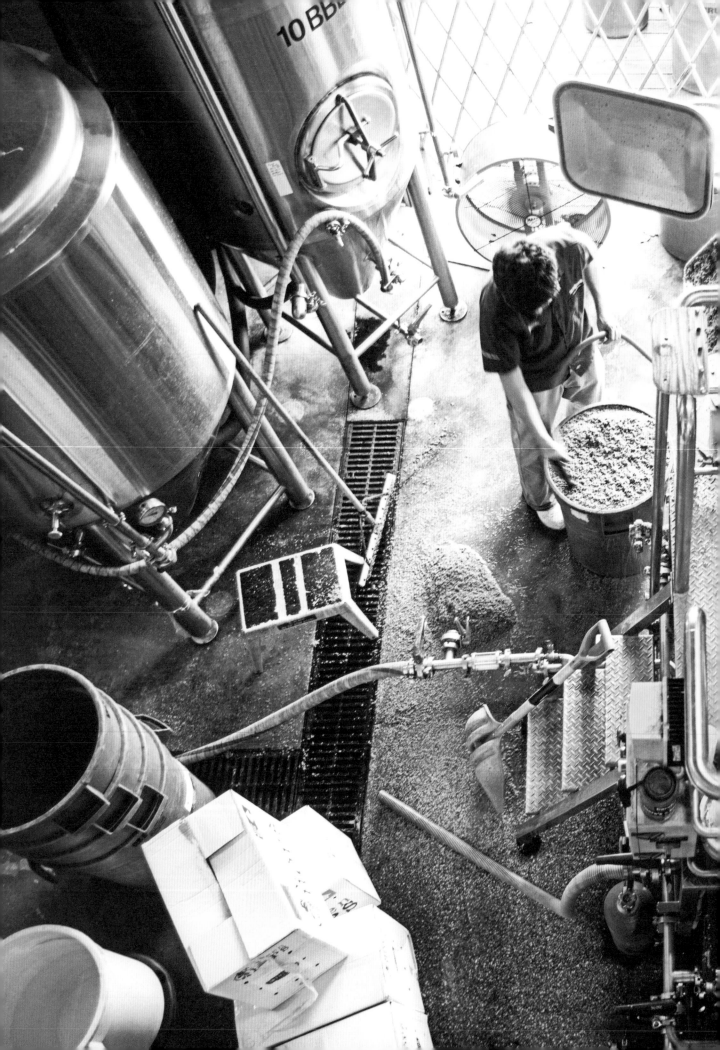

CRAFT BEERSTORY

In just over 20 years, a notable cultural shift in how America produces, consumes and views beer has radically changed the national beer industry. The movement toward locally produced and stylistically diverse products driven by quality and flavor is guiding a segment of the beer world further and further from the swill of massive corporate breweries.

Inspired by the intrepid breweries of the West, the craft beer movement has swept over the states with astounding growth. Now, major craft innovators can be found in all regions of the U.S. and represent a new brand of success: a sustainable, quality-driven beer that can speak for itself. According to the Brewers Association, in 2012, the U.S. beer industry saw a total growth of 1%, while craft brewers saw an increase of 15% in volume and 17% in retail dollars. Although craft breweries are doing well, there's still more ground left to cover; the Brewers Association also reported that craft breweries make up 97% of American breweries, yet their sales share totaled only 6.5% in 2012.

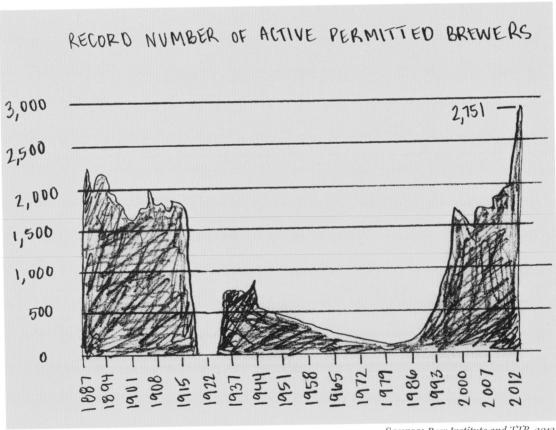

Source: *Beer Institute and TTB, 2012*

A craft brewery, by Brewers Association classification, is small and can produce no more than 6,000,000 barrels of beer per year. Microbreweries such as Intuition Ale Works make up a subcategory of craft breweries which is defined by producing less than 15,000 barrels of beer per year. Due to their size and relationship with the community, craft breweries tend to be involved in local philanthropy, product donations and supporting events. Intuition is a prime example of this community involvement, having donated to local charities and non-profits since its opening in 2010.

Although size is a major indicator of what separates craft from commercial brewing, it is the independence, care and passion of a small brewer that truly allows their product to shine. Craft breweries are normally owned by their head brewers or have less than 25% ownership of an outside party who is not a craft brewer. Without shareholders as the bottom-line motivator, craft breweries are able to maintain integrity and are free to experiment with extreme innovation. The most notable style to develop from the craft beer boom is the brazen American IPA, which is characterized by a strong hop profile, caramel maltiness and considerable ABV (alcohol by volume). These bold American IPAs are now a staple of the craft movement and a prime example of defiance against a commercial industry saturated in pale lagers.

The final distinguishing characteristic of a craft brewery is the ingredients. Craft breweries must have a 100% malt flagship beer or 50% of its beers must be all malt. If flavor adjuncts are used, they must be to enhance, rather than dilute flavor. This is an important division as many corporate breweries substitute portions of their grain bill for ingredients such as rice, which mutes flavor and lightens the color of the beer.

For further reading, we suggest the *Brewers Association* website (www.brewersassociation.org), *Tasting Beer* by Randy Mosher, *Michael Jackson's Great Beer Guide* by Michael Jackson, *Beer is Proof that God Loves Us: Reaching for the Soul of Beer and Brewing* by Charles Bamforth, and the *Brewer's Publications Brewing Elements Series*.

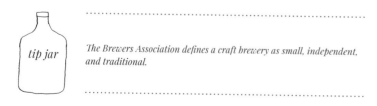

tip jar

The Brewers Association defines a craft brewery as small, independent, and traditional.

THE INGREDIENTS

malts   water   hops   yeast

"Water and yeast are incredibly important ingredients but are often overlooked because hops and malt are the most perceivable flavor components"

"Yeast are amazing! The whole brewing process is designed around providing yeast with the tools to do their job exactly how we desire. They take all the sugars and different compounds in wort and create alcohol, carbon dioxide, and a host of other flavor compounds that add to our enjoyment of beer."

"Hops provide acidity and help balance the malt characteristics of a beer. Hops also lend the earthy, spicy, citrusy aromas to most beers."

"Brewing and cooking are alike: the quality of the ingredients determines the quality of the final product. There's no point in trying to make something tasty from bad ingredients. It always ends in disappointment!"

HOW IT'S MADE

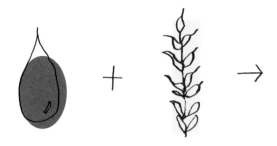

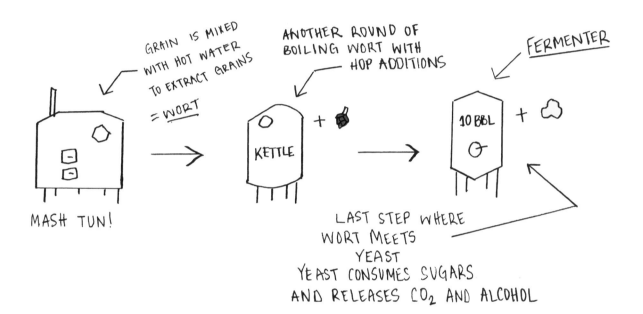

GRAIN IS MIXED WITH HOT WATER TO EXTRACT GRAINS = WORT

ANOTHER ROUND OF BOILING WORT WITH HOP ADDITIONS

FERMENTER

MASH TUN!

KETTLE

10 BBL

LAST STEP WHERE WORT MEETS YEAST
YEAST CONSUMES SUGARS AND RELEASES CO_2 AND ALCOHOL

Ben and I both have a sense of adventure when it comes to brewing and are not afraid to experiment. We rarely use the word "no" when it comes to playing with a recipe and often we have the same final vision for our beers.

I brew towards an idea of what I want the beer to be so I let the beer evolve, tweaking it with each brew, until what's in my glass satisfies what's in my mind. It's great to see creativity and hard work come together in something that other people can enjoy. Beer brings people together to share each other's company, to share ideas, to decompress from day to day troubles, and reminds us that we don't always have to take things so seriously. I like to think it helps us enjoy life a little more.

- Brewer Andrew

INTU TION
ALE WORKS

THE CORE

PEOPLE'S PALE ALE

Style: American Pale Ale
Hop Profile: Magnum, Cascade, Centennial
ABV: 5.3%
IBU: 28
Availability: Year-Round, Kegged and Canned
Our flagship beer is inspired by the hoppy pale ales of the West Coast.
People's Pale Ale has a subtle malt and caramel flavor with crisp citrus
characteristics and spicy hop aromas.

JON BOAT COASTAL ALE

Style: English Golden Ale
Hop Profile: Magnum
ABV: 4.5%
IBU: 20
Availability: Year-Round, Kegged and Canned
This straw-colored ale is crisp, malty and perfectly refreshing. With subtle
bitterness and a fruity aroma, this sessionable brew goes hand-in-hand
with the Florida outdoors.

I-10 IPA

Style: American IPA
Hop Profile: Columbus, Summit, Cascade, Centennial
ABV: 6.75%
IBU: 55
Availability: Year-Round, Kegged and Canned
The West Coast comes to Jacksonville with this true India Pale Ale, featuring
four varieties of hops to create a tasty, copper-colored ale with explosive
resiny flavors and aromas. Our two-row malted barley and caramel malt
come to life with a ?@!#-ton of Northwest hops. It's music to your nose.

KING STREET STOUT

Style: Imperial Stout
Hop Profile: Magnum
ABV: 9%
IBU: 35
Availability: Year-Round, Kegged
Our classic Imperial stout fit for a king. This brew highlights a variety of
roasted and caramel malts, creating a complex and hearty ale with notes of
chocolate and coffee.

tip jar

*ABV is the abbreviation for "alcohol by volume" and represents
the percentage of alcohol (ethanol) in an alcoholic beverage.*

SESSION SAISON

Style: Saison
Brewed in the style of traditional farmhouse ale, our Session Saison is an earthy and crisp table Saison with just the right amount of Belgian funk!

HONEY BADGER

Style: Specialty Saison
A taproom favorite, this Saison has the best of two worlds, showcasing aggressive hops upfront and relaxing into a lingering bitter sweetness from honeyed malts. This tasty brew has true honey badger swagger.

BELGIAN WIT BIER

Style: Witbier
A light and refreshing Belgian wit with hints of coriander and citrus.

BELGIAN HOPPY BLONDE

Style: Belgian Blond Ale
A true bubbly blonde, with a spunky, bright character and plenty of hops to back it up.

IRISH IPA

Style: English IPA
An old-world IPA brewed with English malt and hops for a clean, smooth hop flavor and dry finish.

RIVERSIDE RED

Style: American Amber Ale
A sassy red, aggressively hopped and brewed with two-row malted barley, caramel malt and chocolate malt to tame its temper.

SHOTGUN SHACK

Style: Black American Rye
A black American rye ale with hints of pine needles, roasted malts and spicy green peppercorns. This sessionable, yet full-bodied beer is brewed with 30% malted German rye.

tip jar

....

The term "session beer" describes well balanced brews with clean finishes and low ABV (less than 5%). These brews are fantastic for longer drinking sessions or for drinkers who want the robust taste of craft without concern of intoxication.

....

LIVER KICK

Style: Black Imperial IPA
A fall-time favorite, this Imperial Black IPA has a strong hop bouquet and front-end bite, but leaves behind a smooth, chocolate finish, revealing flavors of burnt toffee and caramel.

TRUCK STOP STOUT

Style: American Specialty Stout
Brewer Andrew's baby. Our breakfast stout is brewed with heavily smoked malts and smoothed out with pure maple syrup and locally-roasted Bold Bean Coffee. It's breakfast in a glass.

SEASONAL ALES

EL GUAPO MEXICAN LAGER

Style: Vienna-style Lager
Availability: May
A Cinco De Mayo inspired beer brewed with Vienna and German Pilsner malts and German bittering hops to create a crisp and mildly sweet sessionable beer.

REDMAN

Style: Irish Red Ale
Availability: March-April
Brewed annually for St. Patrick's Day, this sessionable beer is smooth and enjoyable, malty and lightly hopped.

EL JEFE HEFEWEIZEN

Style: Weizen/Weissbier
Availability: September-October
An Oktoberfest necessity, our Hefeweizen features traditional banana and clove aromas and flavor. El Jefe is brewed with German Malted Wheat and German Pilsner malt to craft a smooth and slightly sweet Bavarian wheat beer.

OKTOBERFEST

Style: Oktoberfest
Availability: September-October
Our seasonal Oktoberfest brew is a rich amber-colored, medium bodied lager with toasty malts and a balanced noble hop profile.

ANNIVERSARY IPA

Style: American IPA
Availability: November
Our Anniversary IPA will excite any hop-head palate. We brew our annual IPA with some of our favorite hops and then kick it up a notch with multiple series of dry-hopping. It's the best birthday ever... every year.

PUNK MONK DUBBEL

Style: Belgian Dubbel
Availability: October-?
Our seasonal Belgian-style dubbel pumpkin beer featuring hints of nutmeg, cinnamon and allspice. Aged on vanilla beans for 10 days, tapped, then gone in flash.

UNDERDARK

Style: Wood-Aged Beer
Availability: February
Our legendary bourbon-barrel aged Imperial Stout. We age our King Street Stout in bourbon barrels for up to a year, blend them with fresh stout batches and then bottle the beast. The Underdark is an epic adventure, not for the weak hearted.

tip jar

IBU is the abbreviation for "International Bittering Units."
This number represents the measurable bitterness of a beer as contributed by the alpha acids in hops.

IBU GUIDE:
< 20 IBU – little to no hop presence
20-45 IBU – notable but moderate hop presence
> 45 IBU – heavy hop presence, intense bitterness

PERFECT POURS

Pairing Food with Beer

Craft beer is earning its rightful place at the dinner table as a favorable pairing companion for everything from fried food to fine dining. Due to an endless range of styles, complexities of yeast character and boundless hop and malt flavor profile combinations, beer is unmatched for its pairing abilities with food. It has the unique ability to match any dish, from appetizer to dessert. Beer is a natural palate cleanser because sipping the carbonated beverage between bites allows the diner to experience the full flavors of the dish with every taste. It is truly the perfect pairing partner.

There are no absolute rules for pairing food with beer. The ultimate taste test happens on your palate. However, we've put together some general guidelines to help you get started. Mix and match, be daring, take notes on what you liked and share your treasured finds with friends.

Pairing Guidelines

Think of beer as another element in the dish. The term "liquid bread" is often used when discussing beer and is an expression we find helpful when envisioning a potential pairing. Think of your brew as bread in a glass (with a longer shelf-life!) and base your pairing on finding complimentary tastes or balancing contrasts.

One pairing technique is harmonizing the intensity of the dish with that of the beer. If you are enjoying a hearty meal, a robust beer with a heavy mouthfeel could pair well; for example, a sirloin steak with an Imperial IPA. If you're enjoying lighter fare, as in a leafy summer salad, a refreshing weizen or lightly hopped ale could be suitable.

It's also rewarding to embrace the similarities between the plate and beer. A naturally sweet dish with fruits could be excellent alongside a Lambic or Belgian Tripel, beers that have fruity and flowery esters and lots of carbonation and spark. If you're enjoying a rich, chocolaty dessert, a dark, roasty beer would complement the plate's flavors. To add more zing to an already hot dish, such as curry, pair with the spicy hop kick of an IPA.

Contrasting flavors can also create an eclectic tasting experience. For example, instead of using that IPA to kick up the heat in a curry, you can smooth it out with a sweeter, malt heavy beverage, like a Belgian Dubbel or Scotch Ale.

Belgian varieties and American Pales are classic pairing partners for just about any dish. When in doubt, these styles make great accompaniments to pretty much everything under the sun.

Beer is more complex than wine and allows for more options when paired with food and used as a cooking ingredient.

Tasting Beer

Beer satisfies more than just our taste buds. We first devour the bubbly brew with our eyes, soaking in all the sensorial promises of a perfectly presented beer. From light straw to resilient copper to opaque black and beyond, the color spectrum is vast and beautiful. Then our sense of smell kicks in; it is the greatest single informant to our sense of taste and is vastly underappreciated. Before a single sip, your nose can identify the intensity of the hops, the heaviness of grains and the spark of the yeast. The beer world offers a seemingly endless array of beer styles, with new inventive hybrids and brewing techniques continuously emerging. The brew before you has all kinds of precious and unique characteristics and quirks to discover and enjoy as they come together to make a palpable whole.

Tasting 1, 2, 3

Hold your glass up to light to observe and appreciate the beer's color and clarity. Beers take on an extensive range of compositions, revealing their grain bill, filtration (or lack thereof) and sometimes even their specialty ingredients..

Swirl the glass slightly to stir its aromas. Now breathe it in. What do you smell? Some beers tote fragrant hop aromas that may release an earthy, piney or even citrus-like nose. Other brews, notably Belgians, can have fruity or floral esters and peppery phenols present. Darker beers which highlight their malts can have a roasted, chocolate or coffee bouquet. Can you identify any of the ingredients the brewer mentions using? Some seasonal or specialty beers may have additions of vanilla, licorice, honey, fruits or herbs. If the beer has been barrel aged, can you pick up on the barrel's previous alcohol, such as rum, whiskey or wine?

The time to taste has come. Take a sip and gently roll the beer around your tongue before swallowing. The carbonation from this first sip will act as a natural sponge and aid in cleansing your palate. Take a second taste, pull in a little oxygen to aerate the beer and savor it over your tongue for a moment. What are its standout features? Does the carbonation pop and tickle? Is it flat and smooth? Is the brew hoppy, roasted, biscuity, nutty or with hints of caramel or chocolate? Note its aftertaste. Does it leave or linger? Most importantly, was the overall impression enjoyable?

Once you've given the beer an appropriate sensorial sampling, have another taste, enjoy, and repeat. You've earned it and heck, that's why the brewer put so much love into it.

tip jar

....
Steps to making the perfect pour:
....

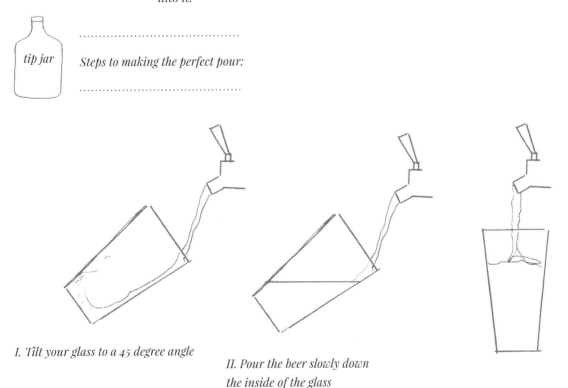

I. Tilt your glass to a 45 degree angle

II. Pour the beer slowly down the inside of the glass

III. When glass is ½-3/4 full, turn upright and pour beer in the center

SERVING AND STORAGE

Beers are complex creations, artfully and consciously designed with care by their brewers. We believe every thoughtful beer deserves our respect and proper appreciation. This chapter touches on serving and storage guidelines which will assist you in enjoying any brew to its fullest.

VISUAL GLASSWARE GUIDE!

Shaker Pint   *Tulip Pint*   *Nonic Pint*

Snifter   *Stemmed Tulip*   *Goblet*

Opposing popular myth: *Do not freeze your mug or pint glass! Ice cold beer numbs your senses and should only be used as a last resort if being forced to drink terrible beer. Good beer will become more complex and reveal enhanced flavors as it warms. Pour into a room temperature glass, recently spritzed with cold water to ensure proper serving temperature, to help form and maintain a frothy head and to allow lacing of the beer as the glass is emptied.*

Serving temperature of a beer:
45-55°

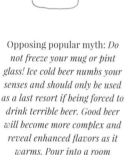

Choosing Proper Glassware

In most American bars and restaurants, the standard shaker pint glass is used for all beers, regardless of style. Although pint glasses are not terrible infractions, they don't do justice to the beer. Choosing the right glassware will allow for aeration and carbonation release, resonant aromatics, and the appropriate serving portion, resulting in the best possible experience for the taster.

When in doubt, we recommend using a stemmed tulip glass, a glass with a curved belly and flared top. This is the perfect go-to glass for head and aroma retention and temperature control (when using a grip or stemmed glass, less heat transfer occurs between our bodies and the beer).

Ultimately, any clean glass will do, but when a beer is served in complimentary glassware, it can ignite the senses and transform the experience of the drinker.

Cellaring and Aging Beer

Cellaring a good beer can be a fun and incredibly rewarding adventure. An aged beer will share new flavor profiles as it evolves from year to year – which is why many beer enthusiasts choose to age multiple bottles of the same year and enjoy them at intervals to note the beer's evolution. To cellar beer, we recommend using a cool, dry place with minimal temperature fluctuation.

Particular styles better lend themselves to the conditions of aging; generally speaking, beers around 7% ABV and above are best (with the unique exception of Lambics and sour Belgians). Although hops are a natural preservative, we don't suggest aging IPAs because the hops lose their robust flavor and characteristics over time. When beers age, the carbonation and hops mute over time, allowing other unique essences of the beer to emerge and become more prominent.

The following are some beer styles that, in our experience, can age well:

Be sure to visit Intuition's taproom in February, during our annual release of Underdark, a bourbon barrel aged imperial stout. This beer is fantastic when consumed fresh, but we're also looking forward to experiencing this big brew mature over the years as new characteristics awaken that were previously dormant in its depths.

STYLES AGING GUIDE

2 YRS — BELGIAN DUBBEL
BELGIAN TRIPEL
5 YRS — IMPERIAL ALES
SCOTCH ALES
10 YRS — BELGIAN QUADS
GUEZE, LAMBICS, + SOURS
BARLEY WINE / OLD ALE
20 YRS — IMPERIAL STOUT

Remember, this chart serves only as a guideline; some brands within these categories will not be conducive to aging. A safe and optimal aging time for most of these styles is between 1-2 years. For the patient and daring, there are savory surprises and quiescent flavors that will become perceptible over longer periods of time. To reduce guessing, some brewers even suggest cellaring times on their package labeling. Experimenting with your own cellaring schedules for different styles and breweries will reveal your personal preferences.

"*In general, beers for aging should be bottle conditioned or, at the least, not filtered or centrifuged. The yeast in the bottle is what makes the changes over time. Also, they help to minimize oxidation which can ruin beer over time.*"

"*There's always a new opportunity to be creative. Whether it is recipe formulation or troubleshooting, brewing is never boring!*"

"*Barrel aged beers create a whole new range of flavor compositions. We're inspired by the endless stylistic possibilities of beer.*"

APPETIZERS
&
LIBATIONS

JON BOAT BOILED SHRIMP WITH FLORIDA ORANGE & ARBOL CHILE

Chris Dickerson, *Corner Taco*

SERVES 2

6 – 12 ounce cans
    Jon Boat Coastal Ale
1 Florida orange, quartered
1/2 lemon
1 dried arbol chile
2 bay leaves
2 teaspoons hot smoked paprika
1 sprig fresh thyme
1 teaspoon mustard seeds
2 teaspoons celery salt
Kosher salt (enough so that the
    liquid has the salinity
    of the ocean)
1 pound large shell-on Mayport
    shrimp (they are sweeter
    and have a sense of
    somewhere-ness)

A local food truck hero offers this recipe featuring Florida citrus, Mayport shrimp and Jon Boat Coastal Ale. It's a truly local dish that will make you feel like your toes are in the sand at any time of the year.

Pour beer into a 4 quart pot with a heavy bottom (preferably enameled cast iron). Squeeze orange and lemon into beer, toss orange and lemon into pot along with chile, bay leaves, paprika, thyme, mustard seeds, celery salt and kosher salt and bring to a rolling boil over high heat.

Add shrimp, making sure the liquid covers the shrimp by about two inches.

The shrimp should be perfectly cooked the moment the liquid returns to a boil –about 3 to 5 minutes.

Do not overcook. The shrimp is perfectly cooked when the tail is curled about 1/4 of the way toward the head. The shrimp is overcooked if the tail and head touch.

Serve immediately, using the cooking liquid (court bouillon) for dipping.

Alternatively, serve shrimp chilled: Strain and reserve the court bouillon and cool shrimp quickly in an ice-water bath. Chill shrimp overnight (or at least 6 hours) and serve with reheated court bouillon.

LEFTY'S CUCUMBER SAISON

Eric "Lefty" Saple, *Grape & Grain Exchange*

YIELDS 1 COCKTAIL

4-5 thinly sliced cucumber wheels
a pinch of fresh dill
1/2 ounce simple syrup
1 ½ ounces vodka
1/2 ounce lemon juice
1/2 ounce Elderflower liqueur
½ a cup or so of Session Saison

Lefty likes the Session Saison because it's light, effervescent, refreshing and picks up flavors well. Basil and cucumber make this a fresh thirst-quencher.

Combine cucumber, dill and simple syrup in a mixing glass and muddle them together.

Add vodka, lemon juice and Elderflower liqueur in same mixing glass.

Shake and strain into a standard 16-ounce pint glass.

Top with beer and enjoy!

SAISON-BRAISED OYSTER MUSHROOMS WITH CORN MILK REDUCTION & HERBS

Sean Sigmon, *Dig Foods*

SERVES 4 AS A SIDE

4 ears of corn
2 quarts of water
¼ cup pine nuts, lightly toasted
2 tablespoons grapeseed oil
8 ounces local oyster mushrooms
2 cups Rye Saison, Honey Badger
    or Duuuvaaal (your choice)
Celery Crudo (see recipe below)
Your favorite chopped herbs, such
    as chervil, to garnish
Salt and pepper, to taste

Celery Crudo:

¼ cup celery, thinly sliced
⅛ cup red onion, thinly sliced
Juice and zest of ½ a
    lemon
1 teaspoon agave
½ teaspoon grapeseed oil
Salt and pepper

This is a classy and unique side dish blending local oyster mushrooms with corn and beer. The flavors are slowly reduced to bring out their intensity.

To make the corn milk, remove corn from cob and set kernels aside. Cover cobs with water in a small stock pot. Bring to a boil then simmer for 45 minutes. Remove cobs and reduce corn stock to 2 cups. Blend 1/2 the corn (reserve the other half for another use), corn stock and pine nuts in a blender. Strain and season with salt and pepper.

Heat a skillet over medium high heat. Add oil and a pinch of salt. Brown mushrooms on both sides. Add beer and simmer until mushrooms are soft and liquid has reduced to nearly a syrup.

Pour corn milk into a shallow dish, top with mushrooms and Celery Crudo and garnish with your favorite herbs.

To make celery crudo:

Mix all ingredients in a small bowl.

LEMLEM SALAD

Karen Hutcheson

SERVES 4

For salad dressing:

¼ cup non-dairy alternative to
    mayonnaise
2 tablespoons Riverside Red
1 tablespoon berbere
1 teaspoon sea salt (optional)

For tofu:

1 clove garlic
½ onion
1 teaspoon berbere
1 cup Riverside Red

1 block firm tofu, pressed and
    sliced into small squares

For salad:

4 cups romaine lettuce, coarsely
    chopped (approximately
    1 head of lettuce)
2 cups green or red leaf lettuce,
    coarsely chopped
    (approximately ½ head of
    lettuce)
2 cups black beans, cooked** (if
    using canned beans,
    rinsed & drained)
1 cup sundried tomatoes
2 tomatoes, diced
1 cucumber, peeled and diced
1 red pepper, diced
1 green pepper, diced
1 avocado, diced
½ cup green onion, chopped
1 cup non-dairy shredded cheese
    (optional)

"Lemlem" means "to flourish or bloom" in Amharic, the official language of Ethiopia. This recipe produces a spicy Ethiopian salad where crisp greens meet hearty ingredients like tofu, black beans, tomatoes and avocado. Traditional Ethiopian spices in the form of berbere give the salad its kick. Berbere is a complex blend of chile peppers and spices native to the eastern Horn of Africa. The blend includes hot peppers, black pepper, fenugreek, ginger, cardamom, coriander, cinnamon and cloves. You can purchase this seasoning at specialty food shops or online.

....

Make salad dressing:

Whisk together mayonnaise alternative, beer, berbere and sea salt.
Set aside.

Marinate and cook tofu:

Place garlic, onion, berbere, and beer in a food processor. Puree until relatively smooth. Marinate tofu in this mixture for at least one hour, flipping after 30 minutes.

Preheat large skillet over medium-high heat. Spray pan with non-stick cooking spray or 1 teaspoon of oil.

Add tofu slices to skillet, reserving marinade. Cook tofu for 8-10 minutes, flipping often and adding remaining marinade as you cook.

Assemble salad:

Toss all salad ingredients together in a big bowl. Add dressing to salad ingredients and toss together well. Add tofu to the top of mixed salad and serve with a chilled Riverside Red.

**for an additional flavor blast, cook dry (pre-soaked) black beans in equal parts Riverside Red and water.

BEER CHEESE SOUP

Stephanie Christopher, *Grassroots Natural Market*

SERVES 10

32 ounces Jon Boat Coastal Ale, room temperature

12 ½ ounces vegetable stock

2 teaspoons garlic granules

1 teaspoon freshly ground black pepper

1 ounce potato starch, prepared according to package directions (usually 1 part starch and 2 parts water)

32 ounces chicken stock

Canola oil or high heat olive oil, for pan frying

1 pound yellow potatoes, peeled and diced

1 onion, sliced

½ pound shredded cheddar

2 bunches scallions, chopped

Crispy bacon, for garnish (optional)

Jon Boat Coastal Ale meets up with cheddar cheese for a hearty soup offering from Grassroots Natural Market. Grassroots uses and suggests organic ingredients wherever possible for this dish.

In a large stock pot, add beer and bring to a simmer over medium heat. Add vegetable stock, garlic granules and ground pepper and return to a simmer.

Add prepared potato starch and chicken stock and allow to simmer.

Meanwhile in a separate sauté pan, heat about a teaspoon canola or olive oil over high heat and fry potatoes until brown and cooked through. Keep potatoes warm while finishing soup.

In another sauté pan, heat two tablespoons oil over high heat and add onions. Allow to cook until brown and caramelized. Set aside.

Add cheddar cheese to soup and allow to melt, stirring constantly with a whisk.

Pour soup into bowls and top with potatoes, caramelized onions and scallions. Garnish with bacon, if using, and serve immediately.

1-10 MICHELADA

John Preston Moore, *MOJO No. 4*

MAKES 1 COCKTAIL

½ **lime, juiced**
½ **lemon, juiced**
3 **dashes celery bitters**
1 ½ **ounces MOJO Michelada Spice Blend (see recipe below)**
3 **ounces tomato juice**
6 **ounces I-10 IPA**
Smoked salt and coarse black pepper, equal parts (for rim)
1 **ounce bleu cheese crumbles**
1 **celery stalk**

For MOJO Michelada Spice Blend:

2 ½ **ounces Texas Pete Hot Sauce**
1 ¼ **ounces fresh lemon juice**
1 **ounce Worcestershire sauce**
¾ **ounce fresh lime juice**
¾ **ounce dill pickle brine**
1 **tablespoon coarsely ground black pepper**
1 **tablespoon Coleman's mustard powder**
½ **tablespoon garlic powder**
½ **tablespoon horseradish**

When you've partied a little too hearty, some good nutrition is in order. Obviously, some refreshing fresh citrus juice could do wonders. Antioxidants in tomato juice have been shown to heal damaged cells. Your achy bones could use a little extra calcium from wholesome cheese and what could be more virtuous than a stalk of celery? You might not make it to church, but this drink might just get you through brunch on Sunday morning.

....

Juice the lime and lemon into a mixing glass then add celery bitters, MOJO Michelada Spice Blend, tomato juice and I-10.

Rim a 24-ounce Mason jar with smoked salt and course black pepper. Fill jar with ice then add bleu cheese.

Roll the cocktail twice between the mixing glass and a shaker tin – DO NOT SHAKE. Pour cocktail from the mixing glass into the Mason jar over the ice and bleu cheese. Place celery down the inside side of the Mason jar and serve.

To make MOJO Michelada Spice Blend:

Combine all ingredients in a squeeze bottle. Put the lid on the bottle and shake. The spice blend will keep for about a week, refrigerated.

LIVER KICKED MAPLE MASALA KALE SLAW
SERVED OVER PULLED PORK ON PUMPERNICKEL ROUNDS

Florence Haridan, *Conscious Eats*

For slaw dressing:

½ cup Liver Kick
½ cup almond oil or other lightly
   flavored oil
½ cup amber maple syrup
2 tablespoons cider vinegar
1 teaspoon freshly pressed garlic
⅛ –¼ teaspoon garam masala
   (depending on your heat
   preference)
⅛ teaspoon sea salt

For kale slaw:

3 cups kale, finely shredded
¼ cup carrots, finely grated
1 large shallot, finely chopped

For assembling rounds:

24 white Russian toasted
   pumpernickel rounds
1 pound prepared pulled pork
⅓ cup golden raisins tossed with
⅓ cup almonds, toasted in a dry
   skillet on low heat until
   light brown
Freshly toasted and ground
   coriander

This recipe would make an excellent dish for tailgating, dinner parties, appetizers or even as an entrée. The strong hoppy aroma and chocolate finish of Liver Kick is an excellent partner for crispy slaw and savory pulled pork.

Make dressing:

Whisk dressing ingredients together until emulsified. Set aside.

Make kale slaw:

Combine kale, carrots and shallots, gently massaging them together. The heat from your hands breaks down the kale's stiffness and bitterness, leaving you with tender greens bursting with flavor. Don't skimp on the chopping because not having to chew through large chunks of raw kale will increase your eating pleasure. Toss with dressing until well combined.

Assemble rounds:

Start with a toasted pumpernickel round. Spoon 1 heaping tablespoon of pulled pork onto round then layer 1 tablespoon of slaw on top. Garnish with raisins and almonds and dust with ground coriander.

Best assembled less than 30 minutes before serving.

HOT SWEET MUSTARD

Kathy Collins, *Café Nola*

1 cup yellow mustard seeds
1 cup dry ground mustard
1 ½ cups malt vinegar
2 cups King Street Stout, divided
1 cup local honey
2 teaspoons salt

Pretzels, sandwiches, sausages... the list of foods that go well with mustard is almost endless. Here's a mustard that will give you a great balance of hot and sweet. These mustards by Chef Kathy need a week or two in the fridge to allow flavors to meld, so plan accordingly.

....

Cover mustard seeds and dry mustard with vinegar and one cup of beer and soak in refrigerator overnight.

Bring remaining cup of beer, honey and salt to a boil in a small saucepan. Remove from heat and cool in refrigerator overnight.

The next day, blend everything together in a food processor. The mustard will need to blend at least 5 minutes to become thick and spreadable. Blend longer for a smoother consistency. Transfer to a covered container and refrigerate. Let flavors meld for two weeks before serving.

ALE MUSTARD

1 cup brown mustard seeds
2 cups Shotgun Shack Black Rye
1 clove garlic, minced
½ cup apple cider vinegar
2 tablespoons brown sugar
1 teaspoon salt

Love that last mustard but need something with less sweetness? Try this one on a Reuben or anything calling for a hearty brown mustard.

....

Soak mustard seeds overnight in beer.

Place in food processor with remaining ingredients. Blend well for about 5 minutes. Blend longer for a smoother consistency. Transfer to a covered container and let flavors meld in refrigerator for one week before serving.

WIT BATTER HUSHPUPPIES WITH ALE MUSTARD REMOULADE

Cari Sánchez-Potter, *Intuition Ale Works*

SERVES 6

For Wit Batter Hushpuppies:

1 cup coarse yellow cornmeal
1 cup all-purpose flour
2 tablespoons sugar
1 tablespoon baking soda
1 teaspoon cayenne pepper
1 teaspoon salt
Freshly ground black pepper
3 large eggs, beaten
¾ cup Belgian Wit
½ cup white onion, grated
Vegetable oil, for frying
Lemon wedges, for serving
Ale Mustard Remoulade,
    for serving (see recipe below)

For Ale Mustard Remoulade:

1 cup mayonnaise
2 tablespoons Ale Mustard from
    Café Nola
1 teaspoon sweet paprika
1 tablespoon lemon juice
1 teaspoon hot sauce
1 large clove garlic, minced
Salt and pepper, to taste

Beer is often an ingredient in battered fried food of all sorts because the lift from the beer helps the food puff up to a golden, crispy crunch we crave. With these hushpuppies, the beer does double duty to deliver light, crispy balls while flavoring the tender, moist middle. They are perfect for dipping in the Ale Mustard Remoulade.

....

Mix cornmeal, flour, sugar, baking soda, cayenne, salt and pepper in a large bowl.

In a medium bowl whisk together eggs, beer and onion.

Stir wet ingredients into dry ingredients and stir just until moistened and combined. Do not overmix. Cover and refrigerate hushpuppy batter for a minimum of 1 hour or up to overnight.

While batter is chilling, make the Ale Mustard Remoulade: mix all ingredients together in a bowl and chill in refrigerator until ready to serve.

Heat oil in a deep fryer or deep Dutch oven to 325°F. Drop batter by rounded spoonfuls into hot oil and fry in batches until golden brown, about 2 minutes. Remove hushpuppies from oil with a spider strainer, drain on paper towels and serve immediately with lemon wedges and Ale Mustard Remoulade.

INTUITION SOURDOUGH

MAKES (2) 2 POUND LOAVES

For starter:

¾ **cup sourdough starter**
1 **cup bread flour**
½ **cup whole wheat flour**
¾ **cup water, room temperature**

Mix all ingredients together in a bowl and keep at room temp. for 4-6 hours in warmer weather, up to 12 hours in cooler weather.

For dough:

3 **cups water**
1 ½ **cups ripe starter**
2 **cups spent grains from your local brewery, well packed**
3+ **cups whole wheat flour**
3+ **cups bread flour**
2 **tablespoons plus 1 teaspoon salt**
A little bit of oil (to help keep the dough from sticking)

Community Loaves veers off the beaten path by featuring spent grains from the brewing process in this recipe. These grains are a byproduct of beer production and give the bread both flavor and texture. They can be obtained by giving a friendly local brewery a call.

In a large mixing bowl, gently mix the water, starter and spent grains. Add the flour a few cups at a time, using either a wooden spoon or your hands to just incorporate the flour into the wet ingredients. Don't add the salt yet! Let the unsalted dough rest for 20 minutes, covered with a towel. Turn the dough out on your table and sprinkle the salt evenly over it. Knead until dough is supple and elastic, using oil on your hands and the counter top to keep it from sticking.

Place the dough in a clean, oiled bowl. Cover with a towel and keep in a warm, draft-free place. After 30 minutes, gently stretch and fold the dough in on itself. This should be easy if your bowl is well oiled. Cover for another 30 minutes and repeat. Let the dough rise for a final 40 minutes to 1 hour.

Turn the dough out on a table and divide in two. Round each piece and let them rest, covered, for 20 minutes. You can shape them into two 8"x 4" oiled loaf pans but it makes a crustier loaf to bake them hearth style. In this case, round the loaves again and place on cookie sheets dusted with cornmeal. Let rise, covered, in a draft-free place for 2 – 3 hours, until the dough slowly returns a gently made fingerprint.

Place in preheated 450°F oven. After 10 minutes, turn the heat to 350°F. Continue baking for about 40 minutes. Loaves should be a nice golden color and sound hollow when thwacked on the bottom. The internal temperature should be at least 190°F.

Let cool on a rack then remove from loaf pans. If you can wait at least 1 hour before slicing you will be rewarded with a more flavorful loaf with a better texture.

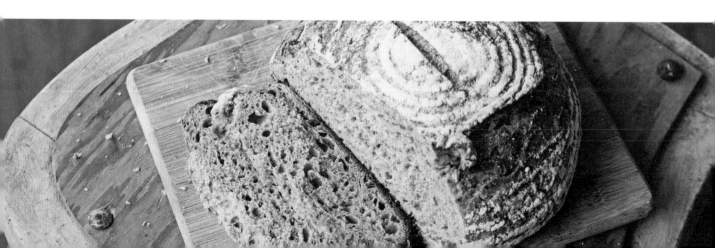

JON BOAT BRAISED DIJON BRUSSELS SPROUTS

Jessica Taylor, *First Bite Blog*

SERVES 4 AS A SIDE DISH

1 tablespoon unsalted butter

1 tablespoon olive oil

1 pound Brussels sprouts, trimmed and halved lengthwise

Salt and freshly ground black pepper

2 to 3 shallots, peeled and thinly sliced

½ cup Jon Boat Coastal Ale

1 cup broth (chicken or vegetable)

2 tablespoons heavy cream

1 tablespoon smooth Dijon mustard (or more to taste)

Brussels sprouts are finally having a cultural resurgence after years of bad kid PR. Folks of all ages have found that sprouts are a real treat if you don't overcook them and you add some great complementary flavors. Here, Jessica brings Jon Boat and Dijon mustard in to pump up a dish that will have everyone cleaning their plate.

In a 12-inch skillet, heat butter and oil over moderate heat. Arrange halved sprouts in skillet, cut sides down, in one layer. Sprinkle with salt and pepper to taste. Cook sprouts without turning until undersides are golden brown, about 5 minutes.

Add the shallots, beer and broth and bring to a simmer. Once simmering, reduce the heat to medium-low for a gentle simmer. Cover the pot with a lid and cook the sprouts until they are tender and can be pierced easily with the tip of a paring knife, about 15 to 20 minutes.

Remove the lid and scoop out sprouts, leaving the sauce behind. Add cream and simmer for two to three minutes, until slightly thickened. Whisk in mustard. Taste for seasoning and adjust as necessary with more salt, pepper or Dijon. Pour sauce over sprouts and serve immediately.

LATTE	EACH	10		3²⁵
AMERICANO		6	WATER	2⁵⁰
AMERICANO		10	WATER	2⁵⁰
LATTE		10/4		3³⁵
AMERICANO		10/4		2⁷⁵

EANS (ESPRESSO ROAST)

SWEET SPOT	COCOA, ALMOND CHERRY, SPICE
ONAL: nduras Micro- Blend	Raspberry, Sweet Cream, Complex Spice
CAF NDURAS	

TIONS

A SHOT	+ 2ᵒᶻ ESPRESSO	.75
OPTIONS	ALMOND, SOY	.35
MADE SAUCE	VANILLA, CHOC, SPICY CHOC, GIN GER	.35
EY	ORANGE BLOSSOM	.50

| AGONWELL MINE PEARLS ANTHUS OOLONG GREY | (HERBAL) • SPEARMINT • CRANBERRY ORANGE • CHAMOMILE LAVENDER | 2⁵⁰ |

THE I-10 PRETZEL

Adam Burnett, *Bold Bean Coffee Roasters*

YIELDS 8 PRETZELS

For dough:

3 ½ **cups bread flour**
1 **teaspoon instant yeast**
1 **teaspoon sea salt**
¼ **cup honey**
½ **cup I-10 IPA**
½ **cup water**

For beer bath:

2 **cups I-10 IPA**
4 **cups water**
3 **tablespoons baking soda**

For beer cheese dip:

8 **ounces shredded sharp cheddar**
   cheese
8 **ounces softened goat cheese**
½ **cup I-10 IPA**

Bold Bean Coffee Roasters' Knead Bake Shop features creations by Adam Burnett. When Adam left culinary school he went to work in an Oregon bakery where he established a love for pretzels. In this recipe, Adam adds I-10 IPA for a soft pretzel which perfectly pairs with a smoky beer cheese dip. Swapping I-10 for some of the water gives this soft pretzel a hoppy, citrus finish that you won't soon forget. If you're tied up in knots about pretzel rolling technique, unwind and simply cut the ropes of dough into nubs for pretzel bites. Easy, cheesy!

....

Make pretzels:

In the bowl of a stand mixer fitted with the dough hook, combine the bread flour, yeast, sea salt, honey, ½ cup I-10 IPA and ½ cup water. Knead the mixture on the lowest speed for 5 to 7 minutes. The dough should be slightly firm and smooth. If the dough is tacky, add more flour, a teaspoon at a time.

Move the dough to the counter and knead the dough for about twenty seconds. Form dough into a ball and place in a lightly oiled bowl. Cover with plastic wrap and let rise for 90 minutes, or until doubled in size.

After 90 minutes, press air out of dough, re-cover, and allow to rise an additional 40 minutes, or until doubled in size.

Preheat oven to 400°F.

Move dough to a non-floured counter. Punch down dough to release air and cut dough into 3 ounce pieces. Allow the pieces of dough to rest for 10 minutes and then start shaping the pretzels.

Flatten each piece of dough then roll each piece with your palms into cylinders about 7 inches long. Once all pieces of dough are 7 inches long roll them out again until each piece reaches 24 inches in length. Form each rope into a pretzel shape and place on a well-oiled, parchment-lined sheet pan.

Boil and bake pretzels:

In a twelve inch pot with high sides, add beer, water and baking soda. Bring to a boil over medium-high heat. Keep an eye on the beer bath as it has a tendency to boil over.

Add pretzels to boiling mixture three at a time. Boil for thirty seconds then flip each pretzel with a pair of tongs and boil an additional 30 seconds. Move pretzel back to well-oiled sheet pan and sprinkle liberally with sea salt.

Once all pretzels have been boiled, immediately place in oven and bake at 400°F for 16 minutes, rotating the pan halfway through the bake. Remove from oven, immediately take off parchment and place on cooling racks.

Make beer cheese dip:

While the pretzels cool, make the beer cheese dip. Combine the sharp cheddar, softened goat cheese and I-10 IPA and mix until everything is evenly incorporated.

Dip pretzels in your beer cheese and enjoy.

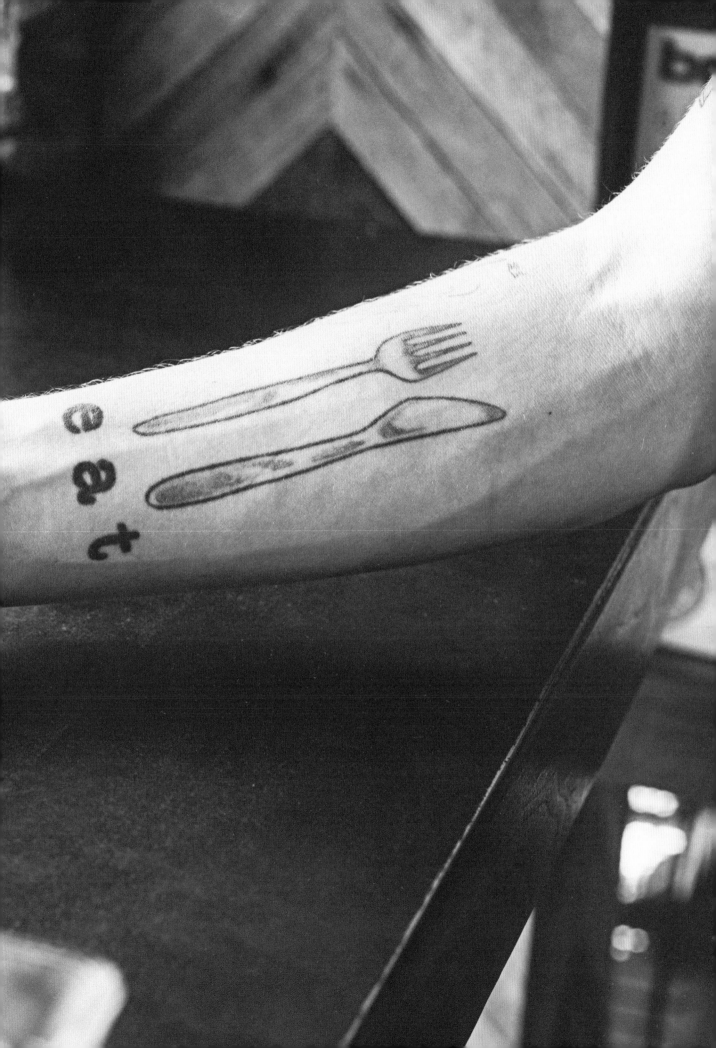

OL' FIDDY FO'S PEOPLE'S JALAPEÑO POPPER DIP

John Williams, *Mug Club #54*

MAKES 24 SERVINGS

15-20 fresh jalapeño peppers
1 pound thick-cut bacon, chilled in freezer for 15 minutes and cut into small strips
6 cloves garlic, minced
1 medium sweet onion, grated
1 can of People's Pale Ale
2 cups panko bread crumbs
4 - 8 ounce packages of cream cheese, at room temperature
4 cups shredded sharp cheddar cheese
1 teaspoon ground cumin
1/2 teaspoon ground coriander
2 teaspoons ground oregano
Tortilla chips or crackers of your choice, for serving

John Williams was crowned champion of the Intuition Mug Club Dip Competition with this delicious take on the popular jalapeño popper. Now you can have all of the gooey yumminess of the stuffed peppers with the crunch of your favorite snack food!

....

Preheat oven to 400°F.

Wearing latex or nitrile gloves, cut tops off of the jalapeños and slice down the middle. Scrape out the seeds and ribs. For a spicier dip, leave the ribs in and discard the seeds. Dice jalapeños.

Place large skillet over medium heat, add bacon and fry until crisp. Remove bacon using a slotted spoon and drain on paper towel. Reserve bacon fat.

Add 1 tablespoon rendered bacon fat back to skillet over medium heat. Add garlic, stir briefly, then add onion; sauté until translucent, about 5-7 minutes. De-glaze with 8 ounces of pale ale and cook for another 5-7 minutes. Remove from heat and cool. Drink remaining 4 ounces of beer.

Take ⅓ of the cooked bacon and chop into bacon bits; mix with 2 tablespoons reserved bacon fat and panko bread crumbs, ensuring bread crumbs are coated with bacon fat.

Mix cream cheese, cheddar cheese, onion-garlic-beer mixture, remaining cooked bacon, jalapeño peppers, cumin, coriander and oregano using a stand mixer or with gloved hands in a large bowl.

Spoon mixture into a 9" x 13" baking dish using a rubber spatula and spread evenly. Spread the panko-bacon mixture evenly over the top.

Bake in the preheated oven until the topping is lightly browned and the dip is bubbling, 10-12 minutes.

Serve with tortilla chips or crackers.

I-10 MIGNONETTE

Ian Lynch, *Ovinte*

¾ cup I-10 IPA

1 shallot, minced

½ English cucumber, seeded, small dice

1 ½ teaspoons sugar

2 teaspoons ruby red grapefruit juice

Freshly ground black pepper, to taste

1 teaspoon parsley, chopped

3 teaspoons ruby red grapefruit segments, chopped

Raw oysters, for serving

A mignonette is a traditional condiment most often served with oysters, as it is here. The citrus notes from the ruby red grapefruit used in this recipe unlock the fresh briny flavor of the oysters while the super-hopped goodness of the IPA lends depth and complexity.

Mix beer, shallot, cucumber, sugar, grapefruit juice, pepper, and parsley together. Mix until sugar is dissolved. Add chopped grapefruit and refrigerate for at least an hour.

Spoon on top of your favorite oysters.

BEER CHICKEN WINGS

Ziming Rao, *Second Harvest North Florida*

SERVES 2

10 chicken wings
3 tablespoons soy sauce
1 green onion, minced
1 small piece of ginger, grated
1 tablespoon vegetable oil
1 – 12 ounce can Jon Boat
     Coastal Ale
1 tablespoon sugar
1 teaspoon salt
1 tablespoon sesame seeds

Why go out? Turn your living room into your own personal wing joint or be the hero of your next tailgating event with this Asian-inspired recipe.

In a glass bowl, mix chicken wings with soy sauce, green onion and ginger. Marinate at room temperature for 20 minutes.

Heat vegetable oil over medium high heat in a deep sauté pan then sauté chicken until both sides turn golden.

Pour the can of beer over the chicken wings, making sure they are covered, and bring to a simmer. Cover the pan and simmer wings for 10 minutes.

Uncover the pan and add the sugar and salt to the wings. Increase heat to medium high and cook, uncovered, until all the liquid has evaporated, about 15-20 minutes.

Top chicken wings with sesame seeds and serve.

BEER CHEESE FONDUE

Wayne Rieley, *Lutheran Social Services*

1 pound cheddar cheese, grated
2 ½ tablespoons flour
¾ cup I-10 IPA
6 tablespoons apple juice
     concentrate
1 tablespoon Dijon mustard
Salt and freshly
     grated pepper to taste
Baguette, cubed, for dipping
Carrot and celery sticks,
     for dipping

It's a universal truth that everything is better dipped in hot cheese. Add some I-10 IPA and you've got a winner. Wayne Rieley shares this recipe for a cheese fondue you'll love. We know you have a fondue pot, but if you'd like to deny it then this dish can be kept warm for service with an electric slow cooker.

In a medium bowl, toss cheese with flour.

Bring beer, apple juice and mustard to a simmer in a medium saucepan.

Gradually add the cheese mixture, stirring constantly until smooth. Add salt and pepper to taste.

Transfer to a fondue pot and serve with baguette cubes, carrot and celery sticks for dipping.

HONEY ORANGE SHANDY

Annie McGuire, *Grape & Grain Exchange*

YIELDS 1 COCKTAIL

1 ounce gin

1 ounce fresh orange juice (about half an orange)

½ ounce lemon juice (about half a lemon)

½ ounce honey syrup*

Three dashes orange bitters

½ a can or so Jon Boat Coastal Ale

Local honey, kosher salt for garnish

Annie shares this very sensual drink which works great with either vodka or gin. She serves hers in a Collins glass. It's sophisticated and sexy, but you won't need to hire a mixologist to get it right at home.

Combine the first five ingredients in a cocktail shaker with ice. Rim a glass with honey, followed by kosher salt. Shake, shake, shake and strain into the glass, add ice, top with Jon Boat and garnish with a slice of lemon if you're feeling fancy. Share the other half of the Jon Boat with a friend.

*Honey syrup: combine equal parts honey and water in a saucepan and stir over a medium flame until combined. Let cool before using.

CITRUS-WIT DRESSING

Heather and Alex Bailey, *Outside the Den*

SERVES 4

1 cup Belgian Wit
2 teaspoon garlic, minced
⅓ cup shallots, minced
    (about 3 shallots)
1 lemon, peel and seeds removed
½ cup white vinegar
½ cup olive oil
1 teaspoon honey
Salt and pepper, to taste
Lettuce, almonds, walnuts and
    mixed dried fruits, for serving

These two local bloggers explore culinary, community and cultural experiences then share them online. They've done a fine job creating a dish which expresses their passions. Local beer, classic ingredients and simple techniques create a dressing you can return to again and again. The coriander notes in our Belgian Wit give an additional depth to this dressing.

Cook beer in a saucepan with garlic and shallots until reduced by half. Pour into food processor, add the remaining ingredients and run on high until smooth. Chill overnight.

Shake dressing well and toss with lettuce, almonds, walnuts, and mixed dried fruits.

JON BOAT COASTAL KALE TEMPURA

Fernando Silveria, *Catering by Liz*

MAKES A DOZEN OR SO

2 cups canola oil, for deep frying
⅔ cup chickpea flour
⅓ cup rice flour
1 teaspoon baking powder
½ – 1 teaspoon chipotle chile
    powder (adjust to your taste)
1 cup Jon Boat Coastal Ale
2 cups panko bread crumbs
Salt, to taste
1 bunch curly kale

Fine fried fancy fare shouldn't be restricted to below-ground produce. Try this crunchy beer-battered vegan wonder at your next party and watch the superfood fly.

Add oil to a deep pot or deep fryer and heat to 350°F.

In a mixing bowl, combine chickpea flour, rice flour, baking powder, chipotle chile powder, beer and panko. Add salt to taste and whisk vigorously until well combined. Set aside.

Chop the woody stems off the kale and tear greens into 1" to 2" pieces. Dredge each piece of kale in beer batter and drop into hot oil. Fry kale in small batches for about two minutes, until golden brown, then remove with a spider strainer to paper towels.

KING STREET STOUT LOUISIANA BARBECUE SHRIMP

Eddy Escriba, *Uptown Market*

SERVES 4

1 yellow onion, chopped

2 celery stalks, chopped

2 medium carrots, chopped

5 cloves of garlic (mince 3 cloves for sautéing shrimp)

12 ounces King Street Stout

1 cup low sodium chicken stock

2 bay leaves

6 ounces Worcestershire sauce

16 large unpeeled Mayport shrimp

3 tablespoon Cajun or blackening seasoning

Oil for sautéing

2 Andouille sausage links, sliced

2 shallots, minced

1 lemon, cut into wedges

2 tablespoons butter

Thick croutons or French bread, for serving

Chopped parsley, for garnishing

Barbecue shrimp is inescapable on almost every Louisiana menu. Over in "N'awlins" the best shrimp don't come from a fancy restaurant, but always from somebody's mama's kitchen. There's no need to be from New Orleans to enjoy this recipe offered by Chef Eddy Escriba. Bon appétit, y'all!

For the broth:

Sauté onion, celery and carrots with 2 cloves of garlic. Once onions are translucent, add beer to vegetables in a pot. Let beer and vegetables cook for 10 minutes then add chicken stock, bay leaves and Worcestershire. Reduce for 15 minutes and strain. You can make the broth ahead and keep refrigerated for up to one week.

To assemble dish:

In a small bowl toss shrimp in Cajun seasoning until they are well coated. In a large skillet on high heat poor 2 tablespoons of cooking oil then sauté the sausage, shrimp, minced garlic and shallots. Once shrimp start to look "blackened" squeeze lemon wedges into the pan then toss in the lemon itself. Let this cook for about half a minute then add 4 ounces of beer-Worcestershire broth.

Allow to reduce for a minute, add butter and allow sauce to thicken with the butter for one more minute.

To serve:

In a small shallow bowl place pieces of French bread or toasted croutons and ladle shrimp, sausage and broth on top. Finish with fresh chopped parsley.

SPICY WHITE BEAN DIP WITH TRIAD TRIPEL

Lindsay Stephens, *Intuition Ale Works*

SERVES A CROWD

1 – 15 ounce can of white beans,
   drained and rinsed
1 teaspoon apple cider vinegar
1 tablespoon olive oil
1 teaspoon sesame oil
1 tablespoon lime juice
2 teaspoons soy sauce
2 tablespoons sriracha
   (or a similar spicy chili sauce)
1 large glove of garlic
½ teaspoon curry powder
¼ cup Triad Tripel
Chopped parsley and chili powder,
   to garnish (optional)
Crackers, pita chips, or toasted
   bread, for serving

There's no reason for your next dip experience to be a snack aisle afterthought. Here, our own Lindsay shares a complex and flavorful dip which you'll be proud to serve at any occasion. The fruit and spice notes of the Triad Tripel play nicely with the mild beans and exotic spices.

In blender, combine all ingredients and blend until smooth.

Place dip in serving dish and garnish with parsley and chili powder, if desired.

Serve with your favorite crackers or toasted bread.

I-10 MARINATED TEMPEH SALAD WITH SOUTHWESTERN QUINOA AND ALMOND-LEMON DRESSING

Stephanie Christopher, *Grassroots Natural Market*

SERVES 2

1 – 8 ounce package tempeh
1 – 12 ounce can I-10 IPA
Canola oil or high heat olive oil
A few handfuls of arugula or
  mixed greens
Southwestern Quinoa
Almond-Lemon Dressing

For Southwestern Quinoa:

½ cup onions, sliced
Olive oil, for sautéing onions
Pinch of cumin
2 cups cooked quinoa
1 cup cooked black beans, rinsed
½ cup roasted red bell peppers,
  chopped
1 cup corn, cooked
½ cup pumpkin seeds, toasted

For Almond-Lemon Dressing:

1 ½ cups almonds
1 ½ cups nutritional yeast
2 cups water
1 ½ cups organic extra virgin
  olive oil
½ cup amino acids
1 teaspoon organic asafetida
  (optional)
½ cup lemon juice, fresh squeezed
  or bottled

A luxurious overnight soak in I-10 IPA gives the tempeh in this salad phenomenal flavor. An easy almond-lemon dressing unites with greens and quinoa for a dish you can feel good about eating. Organic ingredients are recommended wherever possible.

Marinate uncooked tempeh overnight in I-10 IPA.

Heat a lightly oiled grill pan or sauté pan to medium high heat. Add tempeh and heat all the way through.

Place the arugula or mixed greens on a plate and top with Southwestern Quinoa.

Slice tempeh and arrange around quinoa in a sun shape.

Drizzle Almond-Lemon Dressing over salad and serve.

To make Southwestern Quinoa:

Sauté onions in olive oil until soft then season with cumin. Add onions to a bowl and combine with the rest of the ingredients.

To make Almond-Lemon Dressing:

Blend all ingredients in a blender or food processor until creamy.

Note: this recipe yields approximately 1 ½ quarts of dressing. You may want to halve or even quarter it for the salad.

KING STREET STOUT GOUDA WHEAT BREAD

Gary Warren, *Mug Club #53*

YIELDS 2 LOAVES

6 cups whole grain wheat flour, divided (use fresh flour for best results)

4 teaspoons quick-rise yeast

2 ½ cups King Street Stout, warmed to between 120°F and 130°F

1 tablespoon salt

⅓ cup coconut oil, melted and cooled OR vegetable oil

⅓ cup honey (local preferred)

4 teaspoons lemon juice

½ pound to ¾ pound smoked Gouda cheese cubed to approximately ¼ to ⅜ inch cubes (reserve a few cubes once cut for topping the bread)

Bread, cheese and beer — many would say these are the basic elements of life. Mug Club member Gary Warren has beautifully merged the three to create moist, satisfying bread which could almost be a meal in itself.

In the bowl of a stand mixer fitted with a dough hook, mix together 3 1/2 cups of flour and yeast. Add pre-warmed beer and mix for one minute, scraping down bowl halfway through if necessary. Cover bowl with a kitchen towel and allow to rest for 10 minutes.

Add salt, oil, honey, and lemon juice; beat for 1 minute. Add remaining 2 1/2 cups of flour, 1 cup at a time, beating between each cup. Knead dough in mixer using dough hook for 10 to 15 minutes or until dough pulls away from the side of the bowl and feels smooth rather than sticky. Reserve some Gouda cubes for putting on top of bread. Mix in Gouda cheese just enough to incorporate.

Preheat oven to lukewarm by setting it to 350°F and then turning it back off after exactly 1 minute.

Grease two non-stick bread pans, or grease two regular bread pans and line with parchment paper.

Turn dough onto greased surface. Evenly divide into two loaves and place each into prepared bread pans, gently pressing dough into corners. Place a few reserved cheese cubes on top of each loaf.

Place pans in warm oven and allow to rise for 20 to 40 minutes, or until dough is nicely domed above the tops of the pans. Without removing pans from the oven, turn on oven to 350°F and set timer for 30 minutes. Once baked, immediately remove hot bread from pans and cool on rack. Wait until cool to slice. Use a serrated blade knife and slice with quick back and forth motion but not too much pressure downward.

Notes: The recipe calls for coconut oil. It works wonderfully and doesn't make the bread taste like coconut at all. However, you may use canola, safflower or vegetable oil, if you prefer.

Kneading and rising times are approximate and depend on many different variables. The dough must be kneaded until it pulls away from the bowl and is no longer sticky, even if that takes longer than 10 to 15 minutes. And the dough should be allowed to rise in the pans until it is as high as you want your final bread to be.

I-10 IPEACHA

Arielle Coutu, *Tapa That*

YIELDS ONE DRINK

Crushed ice
I-10 IPA (about ⅔ cup)
1 shot peach schnapps
1 orange, juiced, thin slice
    reserved for garnish
Ginger ale, to top off

Chef Arielle offers this supremely refreshing beverage appropriate for the warmer months here in Florida. In other words, keep it handy.

Fill a tall glass with crushed ice, then fill ⅓ full with I-10 IPA. Add a shot of peach schnapps and the orange juice. Top with ginger ale, stir, garnish with an orange slice and serve.

POTATO GRUYERE SAISON SOUP

Andrew Cattell, *Intuition Ale Works*

SERVES 6

1 medium leek, cut ¼ inch dice
    (white and pale green parts
    only)
2 celery ribs, cut ¼ inch dice
2 teaspoons garlic, finely chopped
2 shallots, cut ¼ inch dice
1 rind of Parmesan cheese
1 bay leaf
½ stick unsalted butter
2 tablespoons olive oil
½ cup cream
16 ounces vegetable broth
1 teaspoon dry mustard
64 ounces Session Saison
2 medium Yukon gold potatoes,
    cubed
½ pound gruyere, grated
⅓ pound parmesan, grated
1 teaspoon chopped thyme
    (or to taste)
Freshly ground black pepper
    (to taste)

This potato, beer and cheese soup is brought to a whole new level by the addition of a healthy amount of Session Saison. (These claims have not been evaluated by the FDA.) The beer is earthy and crisp, and the addition of rich Gruyere cheese makes this the perfect fall or winter recipe to fill you up and warm you from the inside.

Cook leeks, celery, garlic, shallots, parmesan rind and bay leaf in butter and olive oil in 3 gallon soup pot (the one you use for homebrewing) over moderate heat, stirring occasionally until vegetables begin to soften (about 5 minutes, or while you cut up the potatoes and grate the cheese).

Once the veggies are soft or a little brown add the cream, broth, mustard powder and 48 ounces of beer, stirring occasionally. Bring this to a boil then add potatoes and cook until potatoes are tender.

Remove the pot from the heat and pull out the bay leaf and parmesan rind. Using an immersion blender (or in small batches in a regular blender), puree soup until smooth.

Return the pot to the heat - high but not boiling - and stir in the cheeses slowly and constantly. Once all of the cheese is melted add the thyme and pepper to taste. Stir in another 16 ounces of beer (or to taste). This will add further beer flavor and also help cool down the soup. Chill the soup and refrigerate overnight to allow flavors to meld.

The next day, reheat the soup and serve.

SOFT PRETZELS WITH PEOPLE'S PALE BEER CHEESE

Benjamin Loose, *Gas Full Service Restaurant*

YIELDS 8 SOFT PRETZELS

10 grams active dry yeast
605 grams unbleached flour
11 grams kosher salt
1 tablespoon sugar
1/8 cup butter, melted
1 ¼ cup water
10 cups water
¼ cup baking soda
1 egg yolk
2 tablespoons water

For People's Pale Beer Cheese:

4 tablespoons butter
1 tablespoon garlic, minced
4 tablespoons flour
2 tablespoons horseradish
1 ½ tablespoons coarse
    Dijon mustard
2 teaspoons Worcestershire sauce
1 teaspoon kosher salt
1 teaspoon black pepper
1 can People's Pale Ale
¾ cup heavy cream
2 cups cheddar cheese, shredded
A few dashes hot sauce, to taste

This recipe helps you step-by-step toward tasty twists of satisfying soft pretzels which will be the ultimate snack once paired with the well-seasoned savory People's Pale Beer Cheese. Don't let the weights and measures intimidate you. Conversions are easily done online if you're not equipped with a scale, but having one is extremely helpful when accurately measuring for baking.

In bowl of a stand mixer fitted with dough hook combine yeast, flour, salt and sugar. Stir together on low speed. With mixer still running on low, add melted butter and 1 ¼ cup water. Continue to mix on low speed until ingredients start to come together. Increase speed to medium and knead until dough forms a ball and pulls away from bowl, about 5 minutes.

Transfer dough to a lightly oiled bowl and cover with plastic wrap. Let rest at room temperature until doubled in size.

While dough rises, begin heating 10 cups water and ¼ cup baking soda in medium pot on the stove.

When dough has risen cut into 8 equal pieces and roll into 18 to 24 inch ropes. You are now ready to shape the pretzels.

Begin by shaping a "U." Holding the two ends, give the dough a twist and lay the ends across the bottom of the "U." Place each pretzel onto a sprayed parchment-lined sheet tray until all pretzels have been shaped.

Bring the water and baking soda mixture to a slow boil and place each pretzel in the bath for 30 seconds. Remove promptly to the sheet pan, brush with egg wash and sprinkle with salt or seasonings of your choice.

Bake in pre-heated 450°F oven for 12 to 14 minutes until dark golden brown. Serve with People's Pale Beer Cheese.

Make People's Pale Beer Cheese:

Melt butter in medium sized sauce pan until it becomes frothy and bubbly. Add garlic and sauté until golden brown. Add flour and cook until absorbed, then add horseradish, Dijon, Worcestershire, salt and pepper. Stir to combine with a heavy wire whisk. Slowly add in beer and cream, stirring constantly. Bring to a boil until thickened then reduce heat to medium. Add cheddar cheese and hot sauce, stirring until melted together. Serve immediately.

ORSAY BOILERMAKER

SERVES 160 GUESTS

Mise en place:

**One 15.5 gallon keg Intuition
Jon Boat Coastal Ale,
well chilled**

**One case top quality American
whiskey (we like small
batch Bourbon)**

While putting together Cooking with Intuition, we've found many recipes appropriate for a crowd. Chefs often cook big, yet so many artisan cocktails are not easily doubled or tripled for serving more than one guest at a time. With this recipe, the Orsay crew solves all your party problems with an offering sure to satisfy the largest crowd.

Have one responsible adult with good judgment start pouring 12 ounces of beer into 16 ounce beer glasses.

Meanwhile, pour 1.5 ounces of whiskey into standard shot glasses.

Instruct the guests to drop the shot glass of whiskey into the beer glass and drink all at once.

MAIN COURSES

DEEZ BEER CAN CHICKEN WITH JON BOAT BARBECUE SAUCE

Daniel Paugh

SERVES 4

Whole chicken
1 - 12 ounce can of Intuition beer
   of your choice
Coconut oil

For rub:

3 tablespoon kosher salt
2 tablespoon brown sugar
1 tablespoon garlic powder
2 teaspoon onion powder
1 teaspoon celery seed
1 teaspoon black pepper
½ teaspoon chili pepper
½ teaspoon cumin
½ teaspoon dry mustard
Pinch of Old Bay Seasoning
Pinch of cinnamon

For Jon Boat Barbecue Sauce:

1 12-ounce can Jon Boat
12 ounces apple juice
3 tablespoons butter
1 cup ketchup
½ cup teriyaki sauce
¼ cup sugar
1 teaspoon sesame oil
1 teaspoon apple cider vinegar
1 teaspoon soy sauce
1 teaspoon chili garlic sauce
1 teaspoon Sriracha hot chili sauce

You'd be hard pressed to find a griller in the land who has not yet heard about "beer butt chicken." It's no mystery why this technique is popular because it allows even the most inexperienced pit master to create moist, flavorful chicken. The beer in the can adds flavor and moisture to the chicken, keeping it from drying out. Because the can keeps the chicken suspended in air, the skin comes out thin and crispy. Crispy skin, juicy meat, beer flavor – add Daniel's savory rub and Jon Boat Barbecue Sauce for a total winner.

....

Combine all rub ingredients together in a mixing bowl. Season the bird by first making a separation between the skin and meat, then putting the rub between as best you can. Coat evenly. (Using a regular spoon will help to separate the skin from the meat and distribute the rub.) Insert your favorite Intuition beer can (open and drink half) right side up into the cavity at the bottom end of the bird. Make sure the bird can stand freely on its own. Spray the outside of the bird lightly with coconut oil.

Fire up your grill and place the coals on one side. Once your grill has reached a temperature of 325°-350°F, place the bird (standing up, resting on the beer can) on the opposite side of the grill from the coals. Rotate the bird every 20-30 minutes once skin turns brown. Your bird is done when it reaches an internal temperature of 165°F for the breast or 175°F for the thigh. Let the bird rest for at least 15 minutes before cutting. Discard the remaining beer left in the can. Serve with Jon Boat BBQ Sauce.

Make John Boat Barbecue Sauce:

Add all the ingredients to a saucepot and stir until combined. Heat over medium heat, stirring occasionally, until thickened. Store in an airtight container in the fridge.

JON BOAT CLAMS

Genie Kepner, *The Floridian*

SERVES 4

2 dozen Florida clams,
    scrubbed clean
8 tablespoons (1 stick) salted
    butter, cubed
1 sweet Vidalia onion, chopped
1 tablespoon garlic, minced
1 inch piece of ginger, minced
½ tablespoon lemongrass, minced
    (look for frozen minced
    lemongrass at an Asian
    Market)
½ teaspoon datil dust, or more to
    suit your heat preference
2 cans Jon Boat Coastal Ale
1 tablespoon apple cider vinegar
1 tablespoon soy sauce
Salt and pepper, taste
1 package rice noodles
2 Florida mangoes, cored and
    sliced into slivers
1 poblano pepper, finely diced
1 bunch cilantro, chopped
Juice and zest of 2 limes

The perks of living in North Florida are too numerous to list, but two culinary bonuses are datil peppers and year-round clams. This recipe calls for datil dust, which can be obtained at specialty spice shops and some farmers markets from St. Augustine to Jacksonville. If you must substitute, use one chopped Thai chili pepper with seeds.

Rinse the clams under cold running water to remove any external impurities; if wild-caught, soak in salt water for up to one hour before cooking.

In a 6-8 quart saucepan, melt butter over medium heat and immediately add onion, garlic and ginger. Stir frequently, until onions turn translucent. Add lemongrass and datil dust, then 1 can of beer. Bring to a simmer and add the first dozen clams. Top the pan with a tight fitting lid and steam approximately 5-8 minutes, or until clams pop open. Remove the first batch of clams to a covered dish and then add another 4-6 ounces beer with the second dozen clams. Steam until opened and remove to the covered dish. Most importantly, you don't want to overcook the clams, so pull them when they first start opening and let them "self-cook" in the covered dish for a few minutes longer.

Bring ingredients in saucepan back to a simmer and add the apple cider vinegar, soy sauce, salt and pepper to taste then remove from heat.

Cook rice noodles according to package directions and drain.

In the meantime, toss together mango, poblano, cilantro and lime in a small bowl.

When noodles are ready, distribute evenly into four bowls, add 6 clams each and a splash of reserved broth to cover the noodles. Top with mango salsa and enjoy!

DUUUVAAAL PANCAKES WITH SHOTGUN SHACK-GLAZED BACON & KICK-A** SYRUP

Tom Gray, *Moxie Kitchen + Cocktails*

SERVES 4

For pancakes:

2 medium eggs
1 cup Duuuvaaal Belgian strong
    golden ale
2 cups Bisquick pancake mix

For drunken syrup:

12 ounces Shotgun Shack
    Black Rye Ale
6 ounces maple syrup
¼ teaspoon ground coffee

For bacon:

8 slices thick-cut bacon
Drunken syrup (see above recipe)

We've long been told that breakfast is the most important meal of the day, so face the morning properly with a well-rounded meal. Pancakes, maple syrup and bacon meet two distinct ale varieties for this deliciously boisterous dish that is good any time of day or night.

....

Make pancakes:

Whisk eggs until frothy in a medium mixing bowl. Add Duuuvaaal and stir in Bisquick. Do not overmix – lumps are okay!

On a hot greased griddle, pour approximately ¼ cup of pancake mixture and cook until edges are set and cooked. Turn and cook until golden brown on the other side.

Make drunken syrup:

Combine beer, maple syrup and coffee in a medium sauce pot. Simmer ingredients over low heat and reduce to desired thickness. The further the sauce reduces the more intense the flavor will become.

Strain to remove coffee grounds. Syrup will thicken further as it cools.

Make bacon:

Preheat oven to 375°F.

Lay bacon flat on a sheet tray and bake until desired crispness. Drain on a paper towel. Using a pastry brush, glaze bacon lightly with syrup.

GRILLED RIB-EYE WITH KING STREET STOUT, MOLASSES AND TANGERINE

Chris Dickerson, *Corner Taco*

SERVES 2

1 pint King Street Stout
¼ cup blackstrap molasses
1 tablespoon dark brown sugar
1 tablespoon tamari (or soy sauce)
Juice of 1 tangerine
1 clove, garlic crushed or minced
Kosher salt (¾ teaspoon per pound
  of steak)
2 bone-in or boneless Rib-Eyes
Extra virgin olive oil
1 tablespoon unsalted butter

Marinate like you mean it with this bold, rich recipe, then go bone-in with your cut to go truly Medieval on your meal. Chris likes to serve his Rib-Eyes with butter lettuce tossed with vinaigrette and local tomatoes, but you can pick your favorite sides.

Mix first seven ingredients together in a gallon zip-top bag. Add Rib-Eyes and marinate in refrigerator for 4 to 6 hours.

Prepare charcoal fire in a kettle grill.

Remove steak from marinade and coat both sides with extra virgin olive oil to prevent sticking.

Sear steaks over medium-high heat until desired doneness (about 125° F for medium rare), being careful to cook for about the same amount of time on both sides.

Remove steak from heat and place on a plate. Place a spoon underneath the steak (backside up) to prevent the meat juices from softening the charred crust.

Spread butter over both steaks, allowing it to melt and mix with the juices. This will become the sauce.

Allow the steak to rest for 10 minutes. Juices that have seized to the center of the steak will redistribute to moisten and flavor the meat. Cutting the meat immediately will cause the juices to escape.

Slice steak along the width into roughly 1-inch pieces and serve with the plate sauce.

THAI DRUNKEN NOODLES

Dennis Chang, *Blue Bamboo*

SERVES 4

1 package wide rice stick noodles, rehydrated

1 tablespoon neutral oil

6 garlic cloves, chopped

4-5 chopped fresh Thai chilies or jalapeños

1 cup ground chicken

⅛ cup fish sauce

⅛ cup soy sauce

⅛ cup seasoned soy sauce

½ cup King Street Stout

1 tablespoon sugar

2 large plum tomatoes, cut into 6 wedges

1 green bell pepper, cut into strips

1/2 cup fresh Thai basil leaves

This can't miss Thai dish gets its drunk on via King Street Stout, but if you make it at home the rest of the growler is for the cook!

Blanch noodles in large pot of boiling water until tender but still firm to the bite, stirring frequently. Drain.

Meanwhile, heat oil in a wok over medium-high heat. Add garlic and Thai chilies; sauté a few seconds, until fragrant. Add chicken and sauté until chicken is cooked through. Add fish sauce, soy sauce, seasoned soy sauce, beer, sugar, noodles, tomatoes and bell peppers. Stir until all ingredients are combined.

Toss with basil leaves, and serve.

29 SOUTH HONEY BADGER DON'T GIVE A SH*T PORK CHEEKS

Scott Schwartz, *29 South*

SERVES 6

12 pork cheeks, cleaned
    of excess sinew
1 onion
1 carrot
1 roasted red pepper
½ green bell pepper
2 cloves garlic
4 tablespoons olive oil
1 tablespoon paprika
1 tablespoon dried oregano
1 teaspoon cumin
1 teaspoon chili flakes
½ teaspoon dried thyme
2 bay leaves
8 ounces tomato sauce
2 cups Honey Badger
1 cup dry sherry
Salt and pepper
Polenta, pasta or whipped
    potatoes, for serving
Chestnut honey, optional

Chef Scotty made this for our "Cooking with Beer" seminar and blew the crowd away. Sure, the title is a little racy, but you'll be inventing new curse words when you taste how good it is. Call your favorite butcher for pork cheek availability or order online.

Preheat oven to 350°F.

Season the pork cheeks with salt and pepper.

Place onion, carrot, peppers and garlic in a food processor and pulse until the mixture is finely chopped but not pureed. Set aside.

Heat the oil in a Dutch oven. Brown the cheeks in batches so as to not crowd the pan. Set the browned cheeks aside.

Add vegetables to the hot oil and sauté, scraping the pork bits from the bottom of the pan. Sauté for about 4-5 minutes then add the spices, sautéing for an additional 2 minutes.

Add the tomato sauce, beer and sherry. Stir well and then season with salt and pepper. Don't worry - the strong flavors of the alcohol will mellow during cooking.

Add the pork back to the pan. Reduce to a simmer, cover Dutch oven and place in the oven for 2 to 2 ½ hours, or until the pork is fork tender.

Skim the oil from the top of the pork and serve on polenta, pasta or whipped potatoes. If you really want to Honey Badge it lightly drizzle with chestnut honey.

BEER AND BUTTER POACHED CHICKEN BANH MI

Alex Leuthold, *Intuition Ale Works*

SERVES 4

⅓ cup soy sauce (low sodium
    if you prefer)
1 sliver fresh ginger
1 stick butter
2 handfuls black peppercorns
1 lemon, cut into slices
32 ounces Belgian Wit
2 chicken breasts (bone in and
    skin on if you like)
½ English cucumber, grated
1 carrot, grated
¼ daikon radish, grated
1 serrano pepper, seeded
    and finely diced
¼ red onion, finely diced
Sugar
Salt
White wine vinegar
½ cup mayonnaise
Sriracha hot sauce, to taste
1 baguette or French bread loaf

This crisp and refreshing Vietnamese-inspired sandwich gets a beery boost from chicken poached in snappy Belgian Wit and rich butter. The tender chicken is balanced out by the crunch of veggies seasoned with vinegar.

Place soy sauce and ginger in a small saucepan and bring to a simmer over medium heat. Allow to simmer over low heat until it reaches a syrup-like consistency, stirring occasionally.

Place butter, peppercorns, lemon and beer in a large pot. Heat over medium-low to medium heat until butter melts and then add chicken breasts. Let stew until chicken is fork tender, about an hour and a half (depending on size of breasts).

In a mixing bowl, combine the cucumber, carrot, radish, pepper and onion. Add sugar, salt and vinegar to desired taste. Place in refrigerator until ready to serve.

Combine mayonnaise, hot sauce and the juice from 1 lemon wedge in small mixing bowl and mix thoroughly.

Once chicken is cooked allow to rest in poaching liquid until it is cool enough to handle. Remove the chicken from the poaching liquid and shred.

Halve the baguette lengthwise and pull out some of the insides, creating a well for the fillings. Liberally spread mayonnaise mixture onto baguette then place chicken, veggies and the soy syrup on top.

MUSSELS AND CLAMS STEAMED IN PEOPLE'S PALE ALE WITH CHORIZO, TOMATOES AND CORN

Sam Efron, *Taverna*

SERVES 2

2 tablespoons extra virgin olive oil
1 teaspoon garlic, chopped
Small pinch of chili flakes
¼ cup of dry chorizo, sliced
½ cup yellow onion, minced
½ cup raw corn kernels
½ cup diced tomatoes
1 dozen clams
1 cup People's Pale Ale
1 dozen mussels
1 tablespoon butter or olive oil
Juice of one lemon
Chopped parsley, to garnish
Salt and pepper

San Marco's own Chef Sam offers up this fresh take on steamed mussels and clams. Chorizo, onion and corn gives the shellfish a Latin twist.

In a sauté pan or pot add olive oil, garlic and chili flakes. Simmer over low heat to infuse the garlic and chili flavors into the oil.

Add the chorizo, onion and corn and cook on low for a 2-3 minutes.

Add tomatoes and season with salt and pepper. Add the clams and beer and bring to a boil. When the clams just begin to open add the mussels and a tablespoon of butter or olive oil. Let steam until mussels open.

Finish with lemon juice and chopped parsley and adjust seasoning to taste.

STEAK BENEDICT WITH JON BOAT HOLLANDAISE

Howard Kirk, *13 Gypsies*

Poached eggs
Hearty bread, grilled
Marinated steak, sliced
    (recipe below)
Jon Boat Hollandaise
    (recipe below)
Cayenne pepper, for serving
Flat leaf parsley, chopped,
    for serving

For Jon Boat Hollandaise:

5 egg yolks
1 tablespoon fresh lemon juice,
plus more for final seasoning
4 tablespoons cold butter, divided
    in to 4 equal pats
⅓ can Jon Boat Coastal Ale, at
    room temperature
Salt and ground cayenne pepper

For marinated steak:

Your favorite cut of steak
½ cup sour or bitter orange juice
    (available in the ethnic section
    of most stores)
¼ cup extra virgin olive oil
¼ cup cold water
3 cloves garlic, peeled and crushed
6 peppercorns
Small handful of flat leaf parsley,
    chopped

Benedict dishes are most often associated with breakfast or brunch, but the addition of hearty marinated steak makes this dish appropriate for any meal.

....

Using techniques that you are comfortable with, poach an egg and grill or toast a hearty piece of bread, such as Texas Toast. Trim the crust off of the toast to have a nice square or rectangle.

To assemble, place the toast down first. Next, place the sliced steak and then the poached egg on top.

Drizzle as much Jon Boat hollandaise as you'd like. (Chef's note: "In my opinion, you can never have too much hollandaise.") Sprinkle with more cayenne or more parsley.

To make Jon Boat hollandaise:

Preparing hollandaise can be a bit tricky, as it is temperamental. Take your time and regulate your heat.

In a bowl, whisk the egg yolks and lemon juice vigorously, introducing air until it doubles in volume. In a sauce pan or small pot (your bowl containing the whisked yolks must settle nicely on the rim of the pan or pot), bring about 1 ½ inches of water to heat, until it is releasing a good amount of steam, but not simmering or boiling.

Place the bowl containing the yolks on the rim of the sauce pan or pot, and begin whisking in the first pat of cold butter. If you see the egg yolks begin to cook too quickly, remove the bowl from the steaming pot and keep whisking until you get the sauce under control again, adding a splash of cold water if needed. Return the bowl to the rim of the pot and whisk in the rest of the butter, one pat at a time, removing from the steam if it begins to cook too quickly.

Once all of the butter is incorporated, begin to drizzle in the Jon Boat a little at a time, whisking the entire time until all of the Jon Boat is incorporated. The sauce may be a bit runny at this time, continue to whisk over the steam and it will thicken. Once the hollandaise is at the consistency you like, remove it from the steam permanently and taste it. Add salt, ground cayenne pepper, and more lemon juice to taste.

If preparing a small amount of beef, place your cut along with the marinade in a gallon zip-top bag and massage well. Place in fridge for 2 hours, massage again and place back in fridge. If preparing large amounts of beef, double or triple the recipe and marinate in a large casserole dish, turning the beef every hour, for a minimum of 4 hours.

Cook your beef in a pan to sear or on a grill, adding salt to your liking. Allow to rest and slice thinly.

INTUITION RYE SAUSAGE

Phoenix Kasten

MAKES 15-20 6" LINKS

Equipment:

Spice grinder
Meat grinder
Chilled bowl
Sausage stuffer

Note: If you don't have a meat grinder or sausage stuffer, many countertop mixers offer attachments which will do the job. Check your owner's manual for these options. Sausage casings can be purchased at many local sporting goods stores or online.

For sausage:

4 pounds trimmed pork shoulder
1 pound fatty pork belly
1 tablespoon caraway seed
2 teaspoons fennel seed
2 teaspoons celery seed
1 ½ ounces kosher salt
1 tablespoon garlic powder
1 teaspoon mustard powder
1 cup Jon Boat or People's Pale Ale
**6 feet pre-soaked natural sausage
    casing**

Phoenix began making sausage simply because he didn't know it was supposed to be difficult. He read a few books, watched a few YouTube videos and taught himself the craft. This particular variety was created for Oktoberfest and incorporates the flavors of the beer and rye for a hearty, satisfying sausage perfect on the grill.

Chop the pork shoulder and pork belly into 1" cubes and refrigerate.

Toast the caraway, fennel and celery seed in a hot pan until they are aromatic and start to "pop."

Using a spice grinder, grind the toasted caraway, fennel and celery seed. (This step is for those who do not like whole seeds in their sausage and is optional.)

In a small bowl, mix together the salt, garlic, mustard, and toasted spice mixture. Sprinkle on the pork and toss thoroughly to combine.

Place meat in a zip-top bag and refrigerate overnight to let the spices bloom and permeate the pork.

Grind pork and make sausages:

Place the pork mix, grinder parts and mixing bowl into the freezer for an hour. You want the meat to be stiff, but not frozen solid. Grind the pork mix using a medium grind into the chilled bowl. The bowl should sit in a larger bowl full of ice to maintain the cold temperature.

Mix the ground pork using an electric mixer on medium-low and slowly add the beer. Mix for one minute – the sausage should look sticky.

Transfer the sausage to your stuffer and stuff into pre-soaked sausage casings according to manufacturer's instructions.

Divide sausage into approximately 6" links by twisting sausages in opposite directions. If you're not confident stuffing your own sausages, the ground sausage makes excellent patties and works well in any recipe calling for bulk sausage.

Refrigerate sausages up to a week or freeze for up to a year.

I-10-BRAISED PORK TACOS WITH MELTED BLUE CHEESE AND CILANTRO SRIRACHA SLAW

Andrew Ferenc, *On the Fly Sandwiches + Stuff*

SERVES 8 TO 10

10-12 6" flour tortillas
2 cups blue cheese, crumbled
Sliced avocado, for garnish

For braised pork:

2-3 pounds boneless pork butt
2 tablespoons olive oil
1 large carrot, roughly chopped
1 Vidalia onion, roughly chopped
3 stalks celery, roughly chopped
3 garlic cloves
2 cans I-10 IPA
Salt and pepper

For cilantro Sriracha slaw:

1 cup mayonnaise
½ cup sugar
¼ cup white vinegar
1 tablespoon Sriracha
½ head of green cabbage, thinly sliced
1 carrot, julienned
Handful of cilantro, roughly chopped
Salt and pepper

Chef Andrew describes himself as a "freestyler" who enjoys cooking with fresh local ingredients. Having a food truck gives him the freedom to expand his creative side. That creativity shines in this recipe which utilizes I-10 IPA to braise the pork featured in the tacos. Chef Andrew says, "The pork takes in all the flavor of the hops in the I-10. You can really taste the beer. It felt like a natural pairing." He's shared this recipe so you can get your On the Fly fix right at home.

Braise pork:

Preheat oven to 300°F.

Place a large roasting pan on the stove top and preheat over medium high heat.

Season pork butt with salt and pepper. Add oil to roasting pan then add pork, searing on both sides until crispy brown.

Add carrots, onion, celery and whole garlic cloves to the roasting pan and brown them as well.

Deglaze pan with beer, scraping up any crispy bits on the bottom of the pan.

Cover roasting pan and cook in the oven for 3-4 hours, or until meat is tender and falling apart. Place pork on a platter and strain the vegetables, discarding the vegetables but reserving the pork jus.

Make slaw:

Meanwhile, make the slaw. In a small mixing bowl add mayonnaise, sugar, vinegar and Sriracha and whisk together. Add salt and pepper to taste. Set aside.

In another mixing bowl add cabbage, carrots and cilantro. Dress slaw to your pleasure.

Note: Slaw can be made a day in advance, although Chef Andrew recommends making it as close to serving time as possible in order to maintain crunch.

Assemble tacos:

Preheat a griddle and place tortillas on hot griddle. Top with about ¼ cup bleu cheese per tortilla and heat just until melted. Stack the braised pork on top of the cheese and spoon some of the reserved jus over the meat.

Top with slaw and garnish with avocado.

BEER-BRAISED SHORT RIBS

Kathy Collins, *Café Nola*

SERVES 4

2 pounds boneless, good quality
    short ribs, trimmed &
    portioned into 5-6 oz. pieces
1 quart King Street Stout
3 tablespoons vegetable oil,
    divided
1 medium sized sweet onion,
    preferably Vidalia, roughly
    chopped
2 carrots, roughly chopped
3 celery ribs, roughly chopped
2 garlic cloves, chopped
1-6 ounce can tomato paste
    4 thyme sprigs & 4 rosemary
    sprigs, tied together with
    butcher's twine
2 cups chicken stock
Pimento Cheese Mashed Potatoes
    (see recipe below),
    risotto or egg noodles,
    for serving

Café Nola consistently proves that the art doesn't end in the lobby of the Museum of Contemporary Art. This short rib preparation will give you exactly what you're craving when you think of short ribs. Dark beer and traditional flavors combine for a rich sauce with a delectable entrée.

Cover short ribs with beer and marinate overnight in refrigerator.

Pre heat oven to 275°F.

Remove short ribs from beer and pat dry. Strain beer and reserve. Season short ribs with salt and pepper.

Heat 2 tablespoons vegetable oil in large pan or Dutch oven. Sear short ribs until brown on each side and then remove to a clean plate.

Add remaining tablespoon of vegetable oil to Dutch oven. Sauté onion, carrots and celery about 5 minutes then add garlic, cooking just until fragrant. Add tomato paste and sauté with vegetables for another 5 minutes, stirring often so the tomato paste caramelizes but doesn't burn.

Add reserved beer and chicken broth to pan, scraping browned bits from the bottom . Add rosemary and thyme bundle to liquid. Place short ribs on top of vegetables and herbs, cover and braise in 275°F oven for 5 hours.

Remove short ribs from oven and transfer ribs to a clean baking dish. Pour in a little of the liquid and cover with foil to keep moist. Remove herb bundle and discard.

Use a hand blender to blend vegetables and remaining liquid into a sauce. Season to taste with salt & pepper and a little more beer if you'd like. Depending on the beer you use there can be a bitter flavor that some folks love but others may want to tone down a bit. If you prefer less bitter flavor, try throwing in a teaspoon of sugar and re-seasoning with salt and pepper if necessary.

Liquid can be strained for a thinner sauce or blended with braising vegetables for a thicker sauce - this is personal preference. Chef Collins bases this decision on what it is being served with. The thicker sauce is great with Pimento Cheese Mashed Potatoes. A risotto or egg noodles would do well with a thinner sauce. Add short ribs back into finished sauce and serve with braising sauce. Short ribs can be kept warm on low heat until ready to serve while any side dishes are finishing.

PIMENTO CHEESE MASHED POTATOES

Kathy Collins, *Café Nola*

SERVES 6

3 pounds Yukon gold potatoes, peeled and quartered
1 teaspoon salt
½ cup milk
3 tablespoons unsalted butter
1 ½ cups Pimento Cheese Spread (see recipe below)
Salt and pepper, to taste

For Pimento Cheese Spread:

½ cup yellow onion
1 jalapeno, with seeds
1 tablespoon minced garlic
2 tablespoons Worcestershire sauce
1 tablespoon kosher salt
1 cup Peppadew peppers
12 ounces smoked Gouda, shredded
12 ounces sharp cheddar, shredded
12 ounces cream cheese, softened

This recipe is a decadent Southern twist on traditional mashed potatoes. The addition of pimento cheese makes this an impressive accompaniment for hearty cuts of meat like the short ribs above.

Cover quartered potatoes with water in a heavy pot and add 1 teaspoon salt. Bring to a boil then reduce to medium heat.

Meanwhile, add milk and butter to a saucepan and heat just enough to thoroughly melt butter.

Cook potatoes until they are easily pierced with a fork. Drain potatoes and add to mixer with whisk attachment. Whip potatoes just enough to get them mashing, then turn mixer off and add milk and butter mixture.

Scrape down the sides with a rubber spatula and turn mixer back on. Mix for another minute, turn mixer off and add pimento cheese. Scrape down sides again. Turn mixer back on and mix until all the pimento cheese is incorporated and potatoes are a fluffy consistency.

Season to taste with salt and pepper.

For Pimento Cheese Spread:

Puree onion in food processor. Add jalapeno, garlic, Worcestershire sauce, salt and peppers and process until you have a well-blended mix.

Using paddle attachment on mixer, add cheeses and mix to incorporate. Slowly pour in the onion mixture and combine.

Transfer to a covered container. Keeps for about a week in the fridge.

I-10-BRAISED PORK BELLY AND OYSTER SANDWICH

Jeff Stanford, *The Blind Fig*

YIELDS 1 SANDWICH

2 slices buttered and toasted
   Texas toast
1 tablespoon Garlic Mayo
   (see recipe below)
2 thick slices I-10 Braised Pork
   Belly (see recipe below)
4-5 crispy fried
   Apalachicola oysters
3 sweet bread and butter
   pickle chips
2 slices of vine-ripened tomato
½ cup baby arugula

For I-10 Braised Pork Belly:

8 pounds pork belly
10 cloves garlic, chopped
2 tablespoons creole seasoning
5 sprigs fresh thyme
1 quart I-10 IPA
1 quart vegetable stock
1 cup Crystal hot sauce
1 cup Worcestershire sauce
¼ cup creole mustard
Salt and freshly ground
   black pepper

For Garlic Mayo:

3 ½ cups mayonnaise
¼ cup creole mustard
2 teaspoons granulated garlic
2 teaspoons fresh thyme, minced
1 lemon, zested and juiced
Salt and pepper

The fan club for this sandwich began with the Salty Fig food truck concept. Today they've evolved into their restaurant space where this sandwich remains a popular favorite. Braised pork belly pairs with crispy fried oysters for a truly gourmet sandwich experience.

....

Slather the slices of Texas toast with garlic mayo.

Build sandwich by layering pork belly, oysters, pickles, tomatoes and arugula on Texas toast.

Braise pork belly:

Preheat oven to 375°F.

Score the fat side of the pork belly in a cross pattern and season with salt, pepper, garlic and creole seasoning.

Heat a flat top griddle or large cast iron pan over high heat. Sear both sides of the belly. Place the belly and thyme sprigs into a 4" deep braising pan.

In a large mixing bowl, combine the beer, vegetable stock, hot sauce, Worcestershire sauce and mustard. Pour mixture into to the pan with the pork belly. Wrap pan with foil and place in preheated oven for three hours.

Remove the pork belly to a cutting board. Strain and save the liquid. (It works well for gumbo!) Cut the pork belly into thick slices.

Make Garlic Mayo:

Combine all ingredients into a large mixing bowl and whip until blended together. Season with salt and pepper.

CHINESE SALT AND PEPPER SHRIMP

Dennis Chang, *Blue Bamboo*

SERVES 4

Neutral oil such as peanut,
    for deep frying
2 eggs
1 cup plus 1 ounce chilled
    Jon Boat Coastal Ale
3 cups cornstarch, divided
Kosher salt and freshly ground
    black pepper
2 pounds extra-large shrimp,
    peeled and de-veined
2 jalapeño chilies, sliced
2 cloves garlic, finely chopped
1 inch piece fresh ginger, peeled
    and finely chopped
1 tablespoon low-sodium soy sauce
2 tablespoons cilantro, chopped
Cooked white rice, for serving

Salt and Pepper Shrimp is a staple on Chinese takeout menus, but you can bring home the crispy deliciousness using this simple recipe from a Southside fusion master (cute paper box optional).

Heat oil to 375° in a deep fryer.

Whisk the eggs and 1 cup of beer together in a large bowl. Whisk in 2 cups cornstarch, incorporating any lumps. The batter will be the consistency of thick cream. Season generously with salt and pepper.

Put the remaining cornstarch on a platter and season well with salt and pepper. Dredge the shrimp in the cornstarch and shake off any excess. Dip the shrimp in the batter, drop into the hot oil and fry for about 3 minutes, or until golden brown.

Remove shrimp to paper towels to drain. Season with salt and pepper and set aside.

Heat 1 tablespoon oil in a skillet. Add chilies, garlic, and ginger and stir-fry for a few seconds, until fragrant. Pour in the soy sauce and 1 ounce of beer. Cook for 1 minute, then toss shrimp with the sauce in the pan. Garnish with cilantro and serve with rice.

BELGIAN WIT-BRINED SMOKED TURKEY

Cole Pepper, *WhitePepper Sports Marketing*

For brine:

1 gallon Belgian Wit
2 gallons water
¾ cup honey or agave nectar
1 teaspoon cloves
2 tablespoons roasted garlic salt
2 bay leaves
½ cup whole peppercorns

For turkey:

1 - 10-12 pound turkey
Sea salt
Pepper
1 white onion
1 lemon
1 clove garlic
1 bunch sage
1 bunch rosemary
1 bunch thyme
2 whole carrots
2-3 stalks of celery

Cole received a kamado-style ceramic grill as a wedding gift and began experimenting with barbecue techniques immediately. He wanted more than the traditional roasted turkey, so he stuffed a bunch of herbs in the cavity along with half of a lemon to hold it all in. Wanting to bring even more flavor to the party, he concocted a brine which features the Belgian Wit to cash in on the fall wheat flavor and coriander spiciness.

Fill large stock pot with ½ gallon of beer. Pour in water, honey (or agave nectar), cloves, roasted garlic salt, bay leaves and peppercorns. Add turkey to pot. Pour in remaining beer. Cover. Refrigerate 12-18 hours.

Remove turkey from stock pot and discard brine. Rub turkey with sea salt and pepper. Cut onion in 4 slices, cut lemon in half, crush garlic with side of knife. Place half of lemon in the cavity, followed by (in order) one slice of onion and then garlic.

Wedge sage, rosemary and thyme into cavity, then wedge carrots and celery to fill cavity and cap with other onion (if room) and half of the lemon.

Smoke breast side down over hickory and a fruit wood (Cole prefers apple or cherry). On the kamado-style ceramic grill, it takes about 1 hour for every 3 pounds of turkey, but it may take longer on a traditional smoker. Garnish with remaining herbs.

EL GUAPO-BRAISED BRISKET WITH RANCHERA SAUCE

Debbie and Don Nicol, *TacoLu*

3-5 pound beef brisket

Blackening season or Cayenne, salt and chile powder or fresh ground chiles

Canola oil

1 quart growler El Guapo Mexican Lager

1 white onion, chopped

3-5 fresh jalapenos, slit down one side

Flour or corn tortillas, for serving

Queso fresco, crumbling, for serving

Cilantro, chopped, for serving

For Ranchera Sauce:

3 pounds ripe tomatoes, roasted, peeled and cored (canned, roasted tomatoes can also be substituted and are available year-round)

2 Serrano chiles

2 large garlic cloves

Vegetable oil

Small white onion, very finely diced

2 inch piece Mexican cinnamon

Salt

Sugar

Debbie and Don from TacoLu share their method for a tender and delicious beer-braised brisket. El Guapo is used here but they also recommend Jon Boat or Shotgun Shack if the seasonal Mexican lager is not available. They say the Ranchera sauce is vital for the tacos, but you can use it for a variety of applications such as enchiladas, huevos rancheros and even as a base for soups.

....

Cut brisket into 2 - 3 inch cubes and rub the seasoning all over meat. Heat a little oil in a large saute pan and sear the beef in batches, removing to a roasting pan as meat is browned. Deglaze the saute pan with beer and pour over beef, almost covering the beef in your roasting pan.

Place in oven and cook for about 3 1/2 hours then add white onion and jalapenos. Continue to cook for another 30-45 minutes, until the meat is falling apart. Remove the meat from the pan and remove the fat from the meat before serving.

Make Ranchera Sauce:

Combine roasted tomatoes, chiles and garlic in a blender and blend until smooth.

Heat vegetable oil in a saucepan over medium heat. Add onion and cook, stirring until the onion is translucent, about 4-5 minutes.

Add the pureed tomato mixture as well as the cinnamon (bundled in cheese cloth or alone if you don't mind removing it later) and bring to a boil. Simmer until slightly thickened (just enough to coat a spoon), about 30 minutes. If the sauce thickens too much before that time, lower the heat slightly and add water, a little bit at a time.

Salt to taste and add some sugar if the flavor needs to be rounded out a bit. Canned tomatoes will definitely need some sugar added!

Assemble tacos:

Pile brisket on tortillas and top with ranchera sauce, queso fresco and cilantro.

IRISH RED ALE CHILI

Chrissy Schneider, *Culhane's Irish Pub*

SERVES 8 TO 10

5 pounds Certified Angus beef,
 ground
3 yellow onions, medium dice
3 green peppers, medium dice
3 tablespoons garlic, minced
3 large tomatoes, medium dice
1 tablespoon tomato paste
2 cups Irish Red Ale
¼ Culhane's House Seasoning
 (available for purchase
 online or at the pub)
3 Tablespoons Franks Red
 Hot sauce
½ cup chili powder
2 – 13.7 ounce cans Heinz
 Irish Beans
Salt, to taste
Sour cream, to serve
Scallions, chopped, to serve

Culhane's has the distinction of having its own Intuition brew, the Irish Red Ale. Like Culhane's, it has a flavor all its own which blends beautifully into this hearty, meaty chili. You may not associate chili with the Emerald Isle, but the Irish Beans and IPA flavor will kick off a bit of a hooley from the hills of Olde Willowbranch to the sylvan shores where Neptune meets the sea. If you don't have Culhane's House Seasoning, roasted garlic pepper seasoning makes a good substitute.

....

Heat a medium pot over medium high heat and brown the ground beef, breaking it up as it cooks. Once meat is browned, drain off the fat.

Add the onions, peppers, garlic, tomatoes and tomato paste to the beef and sauté until vegetables are tender. Pour in the beer and stir. Add house seasoning, hot sauce, chili powder and beans. Stir together and season with salt to taste. Allow to simmer until flavors meld.

Serve topped with sour cream and scallions.

JON BOAT FISH 'N CHIPS

YIELDS ENOUGH BATTER FOR 8 THREE-OUNCE FISH FILLETS

2 cups Tempura Mix
1 teaspoon granulated garlic
1 teaspoon paprika
Pinch of salt
1 tablespoon Culhane's House
 Seasoning
1 cup Jon Boat Coastal Ale
1 cup soda water
8 – 3 ounce cod fillets
All-purpose flour, seasoned with
 salt and pepper
Peanut oil, for frying
French fries, for serving

Jon Boat Coastal Ale lends a hand to the batter in this famous #1 best seller at Culhane's Irish Pub. If you prefer, you can also use it to batter chicken or other seafood. The result is light, crispy and delicious.

....

Mix together the tempura mix, garlic, paprika, salt and house seasoning in a medium bowl. Slowly add the beer and soda water and whisk together until smooth.

Preheat frying oil to 350°F.

Dust the fish fillets with seasoned flour then dip into the beer batter and place them straight into the fryer. Fry for 3 minutes, flip the fish and fry an additional 3 minutes until golden brown and crispy.

Serve with French Fries.

I-10 PIZZA DOUGH WITH ARUGULA, TOMATOES, PURPLE POTATOES & HONEY GOAT CHEESE DRIZZLED IN HOUSE BACON VINAIGRETTE

Justin Pa'ala, *Mellow Mushroom*

SERVES 4

For beer dough:

1 cup I-10 IPA,
    at room temperature
1 tablespoon sugar
1 pinch salt
3 ½ teaspoons active dry yeast
    (1 ½ packets)
2 cups flour
1 cup cornmeal
¾ teaspoon salt
¼ cup olive oil
Extra flour as needed

For pizza toppings:

Cornmeal, for sprinkling on
    pizza peel
½ pound arugula
8 ounces honey goat cheese
1 large yellow tomato, sliced into
    8 slices
½ pound purple potatoes, thinly
    sliced, seasoned with olive oil
    and honey and sautéed
Salt and pepper, to taste
Bacon Vinaigrette

We all know that beer makes great bread, but have you considered it in pizza dough? Beer and pizza goes so well together that it can't help but be a winner. Justin Pa'ala from Mellow Mushroom pairs that beer crust with honey goat cheese, arugula, yellow tomatoes and purple potatoes as toppings, then drizzles the finished pizza with Bacon Vinaigrette. Delectable!

....

Make beer dough:

In a 2 cup liquid measuring cup add beer, sugar and salt. Stir in the yeast and allow to stand for 5 minutes, or until yeast starts to foam.

Add flour, cornmeal, beer / yeast mixture, salt and oil to the bowl of a stand mixer and beat on medium speed with the dough hook attachment. If the dough is sticky or tacky, knead in a little flour. Continue to beat until your dough is thoroughly combined and has gathered into a single mass.

Oil the inside of a large bowl, turning to coat the bowl completely with oil but without having a lot of oil gather on the bottom. Use a paper towel to help distribute oil if necessary. Place the dough in the bowl.

Preheat oven to 175°F.

Set bowl with dough on top of the stovetop right where the heat from the oven would vent out. Cover the bowl with a damp kitchen towel. Justin suggests draping part of the towel over the top back part of the oven and then over the bowl to allow the oven heat to vent into your bowl. This technique will create a warm-humid environment for proofing. Dough is ready when it has doubled in bulk, about 1 hour. About 15 minutes into proofing turn your oven off.

To shape the dough, place dough on a floured surface and lightly flour the top. With floured hands or a bench scraper, cut your dough in half. Shape ½ of dough into circle. With a floured rolling pin, roll the dough out to 3/16" thickness or as thin as possible while still being able to move dough around.

For Bacon Vinaigrette:

MAKES ABOUT 1/3 CUP

3 slices bacon
1 medium shallot, minced
2 tablespoons olive oil
1 1/2 tablespoons cider vinegar
Salt and freshly ground pepper

Assemble and bake pizza:

Place pizza stone inside oven and preheat to 450°F.

Sprinkle cornmeal onto surface of a baking sheet or pizza peel. Add shaped dough to peel. Top dough first with arugula then add goat cheese in small pieces. Place tomato slices around the pizza (one for each slice) and top with potato slices. Season with salt and pepper.

Slide pizza from peel to stone in oven and bake for 13 – 17 minutes, depending on how you like your crust and the amount of toppings you've added. The crust should be crisp.

Remove pizza from oven, cut into 8 slices and drizzle with Bacon Vinaigrette.

Make Bacon Vinaigrette:

Heat a medium skillet over moderate heat. Cook the bacon until brown and crisp, about 10 minutes. Remove from the skillet and set aside.

Add the shallot to the bacon fat and cook, stirring, for 2 minutes until the shallots are translucent.

Meanwhile, combine the oil and vinegar in a small bowl. Season with salt and pepper.

Stir the oil / vinegar mixture into the pan with the shallots and scrape up the brown bits from the bottom of the pan. Pour the dressing into a bowl and use immediately.

ONE SPARK MARINATED PORK CHOPS
Thomas Tolxdorf, *The Ritz-Carlton Amelia Island*

MAKES 6 SERVINGS

6 pork chops, each 5-6 ounces,
      boneless or bone-in
1 teaspoon Spanish paprika
2 teaspoons Dijon or whole grain
      mustard
1 teaspoons garlic, minced
2 teaspoons fresh oregano,
      chopped or 1 teaspoon dried
1 large red onion, sliced ¼ inch
      thick
1 bay leaf
4 ounces olive oil or grape seed oil
16 ounces One Spark Kolsch
Salt and fresh ground pepper,
      to taste
German-style hard rolls,
      for serving

Chef Tolxdorf shares a pork chop recipe his mother made back in Germany. The One Spark kölsch adds great flavor and keeps it moist during cooking.

Season the pork on both sides with salt, pepper and paprika. Spread the mustard evenly on both sides.

Place the seasoned meat in a pan large enough to hold the chops. They should be placed together tightly but not stacked.

Add the garlic and oregano and place the onion and bay leaf on top. Pour the oil over the meat evenly and add the beer. It should cover the meat entirely.

Wrap tightly and place in the refrigerator for at least 24 hours. When marinating longer than 24 hours use less salt. You can always add more salt after grilling. if needed.

For the best flavor, grill your steaks on charcoal. Grill them at low to medium heat until done, about 3 minutes per side.

Rest the pork chops for several minutes covered with aluminum foil before serving.

Enjoy it on a German-style hard roll with a cold beer.

I-10 IPA ROASTED CHICKEN WITH TURNIPS, BUTTERNUT AND BRUSSELS SPROUTS

Ezekiel Mears, *Bistro Aix*

SERVES 2

1 whole fresh chicken

For marinade:

2 quarts ice
1 - 12 ounce can I-10 IPA
2 tablespoons whole grain mustard
1 tablespoon fresh thyme, chopped
1 ½ teaspoons salt
½ teaspoon pepper

For mustard sauce:

6 ounces I-10 IPA
4 tablespoons whole grain mustard
1 teaspoon fresh thyme, chopped
2 cups chicken stock
3 tablespoons corn starch mixed
    with 1 tablespoon water to
    make a slurry (mixture which
    thickens liquid when heated)

For root vegetables:

1 turnip, peeled and cut into large
    batonnet (¾ x ¾ x 3 inch
    sticks)
1 butternut squash, peeled cut into
    large batonnet (¾ x ¾ x 3
    inch sticks)
2 tablespoons olive oil
Salt and pepper
1 teaspoon unsalted butter
5 ounces Brussels sprouts,
    quartered and lightly
    blanched in salt water
Parsley leaves, for garnish

You may not have Aix's sweet wood-fired oven at home, but you can still produce a masterful roasted chicken in your own kitchen. A simple but flavorful beer marinade before roasting brings the deliciousness without the remodeling costs!

Marinate chicken:

Place ice in a large glass bowl.

In a small saucepan combine beer, mustard, thyme, salt and pepper and and bring to a simmer. Allow to simmer for three minutes. Pour marinade over the ice and stir until cold.

Marinate the chicken in this mixture for 24 hours in the refrigerator.

Make mustard sauce:

In a medium sauce pot simmer beer, mustard, thyme and chicken stock.

Reduce sauce by half then whisk in corn starch slurry to thicken. Keep warm while preparing chicken and vegetables.

Make root vegetables:

Preheat oven to 350°F degrees.

Lightly toss turnip and butternut squash in olive oil and season with salt and pepper. Place on a baking tray and roast until tender.

Heat butter in a small sauté pan and warm Brussels sprouts in pan until hot.

Roast chicken:

Place chicken in a roasting pan and roast at 350°F until it reaches an internal temperature of 165°F.

Carve and serve aside a stack of roasted root vegetables and Brussels sprouts. Pour mustard sauce over the finished chicken and garnish with parsley leaves.

ALE BRINED SCALLOP SALAD WITH KING STREET REDUCTION SAUCE

Ron Block, *WJXT*

SERVES 4 TO 5

For brine:

12 ounces People's Pale Ale
2 tablespoons salt
1 cup water
¼ cup lemon juice
12 to 15 medium scallops
    (dry packed preferred)
Freshly ground black pepper
2 tablespoons olive oil
2 tablespoons butter

For sauce:

1 cup King Street Stout
1 tablespoon molasses
3 tablespoons balsamic vinegar
1 tablespoon soy sauce

For salad:

¼ cup quinoa
Vegetable oil, for frying
Kosher salt and freshly
    ground black pepper
Arugula
Avocado, sliced in wedges
Heirloom tomatoes,
    cut in small wedges

Lime and People's Pale jazz up the marinade for the scallops in this creative salad featuring crisped quinoa, arugula and avocado. "Dry packed" scallops are recommended for this recipe because they are not treated with phosphates, don't hold as much water, can be seared properly and are generally firmer and more flavorful than "wet" scallops. Ask your fishmonger, because you can't tell just by looking at them!

....

Brine and cook scallops:

Combine first five ingredients, cover and refrigerate at least one hour.

Remove the scallops from the refrigerator, drain and place on 4-5 paper towels. Place another layer of paper towels on top and allow scallops to finish draining and drying for 15 minutes. Season scallops with freshly ground black pepper.

Melt olive oil and butter in a pan over high heat. Allow butter to melt to a point of just smoking. Add scallops to pan and cook to a dark golden sear, about 2 minutes. Flip and cook on other side until seared. Remove from pan.

Make sauce:

Add all sauce ingredients to a saucepan and bring to a boil over high heat. Reduce to a strong simmer and cook until sauce is reduced and thickened (it should coat a spoon), about 10 minutes. Set aside.

Make salad:

Cook quinoa until just tender in salted boiling water. Drain in a fine sieve and spread on a baking sheet. Allow to cool and dry, about 30 minutes. Heat about ¼ inch vegetable oil in a skillet until shimmering. Add quinoa and fry over moderate heat until crisp, about 2 minutes. Drain in a sieve and spread on paper towels to dry. Season with salt.

Place a bed of arugula on a plate, placing slices of avocado and heirloom tomato wedges on top. Place scallops on top and drizzle the salad with the sauce. Add salt and pepper as desired.

SPICY VEGETARIAN CHILI WITH KING STREET STOUT AND JON BOAT JALAPEÑO CORN BREAD

Gary Dunkle, *Kickbacks Gastropub*

SERVES 12

For chili:

3 tablespoons olive oil
1 white onion, chopped
1 red bell pepper, chopped
1 green bell pepper, chopped
1 jalapeño pepper, seeded and
    chopped
8 cloves garlic, chopped
1 chipotle pepper in adobo,
    chopped
1 tablespoon adobo sauce from can
    of chipotles in adobo
1 – 14 ounce can green chilies
2 tablespoons cumin
2 tablespoons chili powder
1 tablespoon coriander
1 tablespoon garlic powder
1 teaspoon oregano, dried
¼ teaspoon cayenne
1 tablespoon smoked paprika
1 pound tempeh, crumbled
2 cups King Street Stout
1 – 28 ounce can peeled tomatoes
1 – 28 ounce can diced tomatoes
1 – 14 ounce can black beans,
    drained and rinsed
1 – 14 ounce can kidney beans,
    drained and rinsed
1 – 14 ounce can garbanzo beans,
    drained and rinsed
1 – 14 ounce can whole kernel
    corn, drained and rinsed
Kosher salt and black pepper,
    to taste
2 cups Greek yogurt
½ cup green onion, chopped
Avocados, sliced

We've all been there. You need a dish for a crowd but you aren't sure about which crowd will be eating it. No matter your audience, this vegetarian chili from Chef Dunkle will please your hungriest tailgaters!

Heat a large pot over medium high heat. Add olive oil and sauté onions, bell peppers, jalapeño, and garlic for 5-7 minutes until tender, but not mushy.

Stir in chipotle, adobo sauce, green chilies, cumin, chili powder, coriander, garlic powder, oregano, cayenne and paprika. Simmer for 3-4 minutes then add tempeh. Stir to coat.

Add beer and tomatoes to chili. Bring to a boil then add all the beans. Return to a boil then reduce heat to low and cover. Simmer for about 1 hour, stirring occasionally.

Add corn and simmer for 5 minutes. Season with salt and pepper to taste.

Serve chili in warm bowls, garnished with Greek yogurt, green onions, and avocado slices.

Accompany with Jon Boat Jalapeño Corn Bread.

For corn bread:

3 cups all-purpose flour
1 tablespoon baking powder
1 tablespoon granulated sugar
1 teaspoon fine salt
12 ounces Jon Boat Coastal Ale
1 ½ cups fresh or frozen corn
      kernels, thawed if frozen
      (about 6 1/2 ounces)
½ cup (about 2 ounces) pickled
      jalapeños, coarsely
      chopped
4 tablespoons unsalted butter
      (1/2 stick), melted, plus
      extra for greasing pan

Heat the oven to 350°F and arrange a rack in the middle. Generously coat a standard 12-well muffin pan with butter; set aside.

Whisk the flour, baking powder, sugar, and salt together in a large bowl until aerated and any large lumps are broken up.

Add the beer, corn, jalapeños, and 3 tablespoons of melted butter to the flour mixture. Stir until the flour is just incorporated - do not overmix. The batter will be very thick.

Using a rubber spatula, scrape the batter into the prepared muffin pan. Top muffins with remaining butter. Bake until light golden brown and a toothpick inserted into the center of the bread comes out clean, about 30 minutes.

Let the muffins cool for 10 minutes, then remove them from the pan and finish cooling on a wire rack.

JAMAICA ME STOUT OXTAILS

Sherri Crews, *Cowford Ale Sharing Klub*

SERVES 4

2 tablespoons olive oil

3 pounds oxtails

2 teaspoons salt

1 teaspoon freshly
    ground black pepper

1 cup onion, diced

1 cup carrots, diced

1 cup celery, diced

2 tablespoon garlic, minced

1 teaspoon ginger, minced

2 tablespoons tomato paste

2 tablespoons all-purpose flour

24-ounces King Street Stout

1 teaspoon cinnamon

1 teaspoon ground allspice

2 teaspoons garam masala

1 teaspoon sugar

2-3 cups beef broth

Dark green end of a leek, washed
    (this will be removed so
    don't cut)

1 tablespoon parsley, chopped

Brown rice or barley, for serving

As a member of the Cowford Ale Sharing Klub (CASK), Sherri knows a thing or two about how to use a good brew. In this recipe, she utilizes the bold flavors of King Street Stout to create a phenomenal oxtail braise. Oxtails are becoming more readily available at grocery store butcher counters and are often found at Asian groceries. Call ahead to ask for availability. To really up the beer flavor, Sherri uses half beer, half water for cooking her rice or barley.

Place a large Dutch oven on medium high heat. Once heated add the olive oil. Salt and pepper all sides of the oxtails. Once the olive oil is shimmering, add the oxtails and brown on all sides. Do this in batches if it is a tight fit in the pot for better browning. Once browned on all sides, remove from pot and place on a plate for later.

Add the onions, carrots and celery to the pan. Stir occasionally until onions are soft. Add the garlic and ginger and sauté for one minute. Add the tomato paste and cook 3 minutes more. Sprinkle the flour over the veggies and stir to incorporate. Cook 3 more minutes. Add the beer and stir. Boil beer-veggie mixture 5 minutes.

Add the cinnamon, allspice, garam masala and sugar and mix well. Place the oxtails back into the pot.

Cover with beef broth until oxtails are submerged by about ¾ inch liquid above the oxtails. Lay the leeks on top.

Note: if you like leeks you could thinly slice them and add now; otherwise, remove them before serving.

Return the pan to a boil and place the lid over the pan. Once a steady stream of steam is emitted from the pan, lower the heat to a simmer and cook the oxtails until tender, about 3 hours. During the last hour, leave the lid slightly ajar to allow reduction of liquid. Skim any fat and discard. Stir in chopped parsley just before serving for color and freshness, reserving some to sprinkle once plated. Serve immediately over brown rice or barley.

The Swinging Bavarians really pump up the crowd with authentic Bavarian dancing, Alpine yodeling, Austrian cowbells and traditional German drinking songs every year at our Oktoberfest celebration!

TOTS-N-BRATS

Constantine Deyneko, *Catering Team*

SERVES 6 TO 8

2 links Bavarian bratwurst
2 links Bohemia smokies
2 links wieners
1 link beef frankfurter
2 cans I-10 IPA
2 tablespoons butter
1 – 16 ounce can sauerkraut,
    rinsed, drained and
    chopped
1 - 10 ¾ ounce can condensed
    cheddar cheese soup
½ cup milk
1 – 32 ounce package frozen
    tater tots
1 cup shredded cheddar cheese
    (about 4 ounces)

Constantine has been the rock star catering our Oktoberfest event for three years in a row. His offering blends all of the best Oktoberfest flavors – FOUR kinds of sausage, sauerkraut, cheese, potatoes and of course, beer. This ain't your mama's tater tot casserole, kids!

Preheat oven to 450°F. Grease a 9" x 13" baking dish.

In large saucepan combine all sausages and beer. Bring to a boil then reduce heat and simmer for 10 minutes. Drain sausages and cut into 1/4 inch slices.

Heat butter over medium high heat in a large skillet. Sauté sausage slices until brown then remove from skillet and drain on a paper towel.

Spoon sauerkraut into greased baking dish and top with sausage slices.

Combine cheddar soup and milk in a bowl and drizzle over sausages. Top with tater tots.

Bake for 20 to 25 minutes or until potatoes are lightly browned.

Sprinkle casserole with cheese and bake 5 more minutes, until cheese is melted.

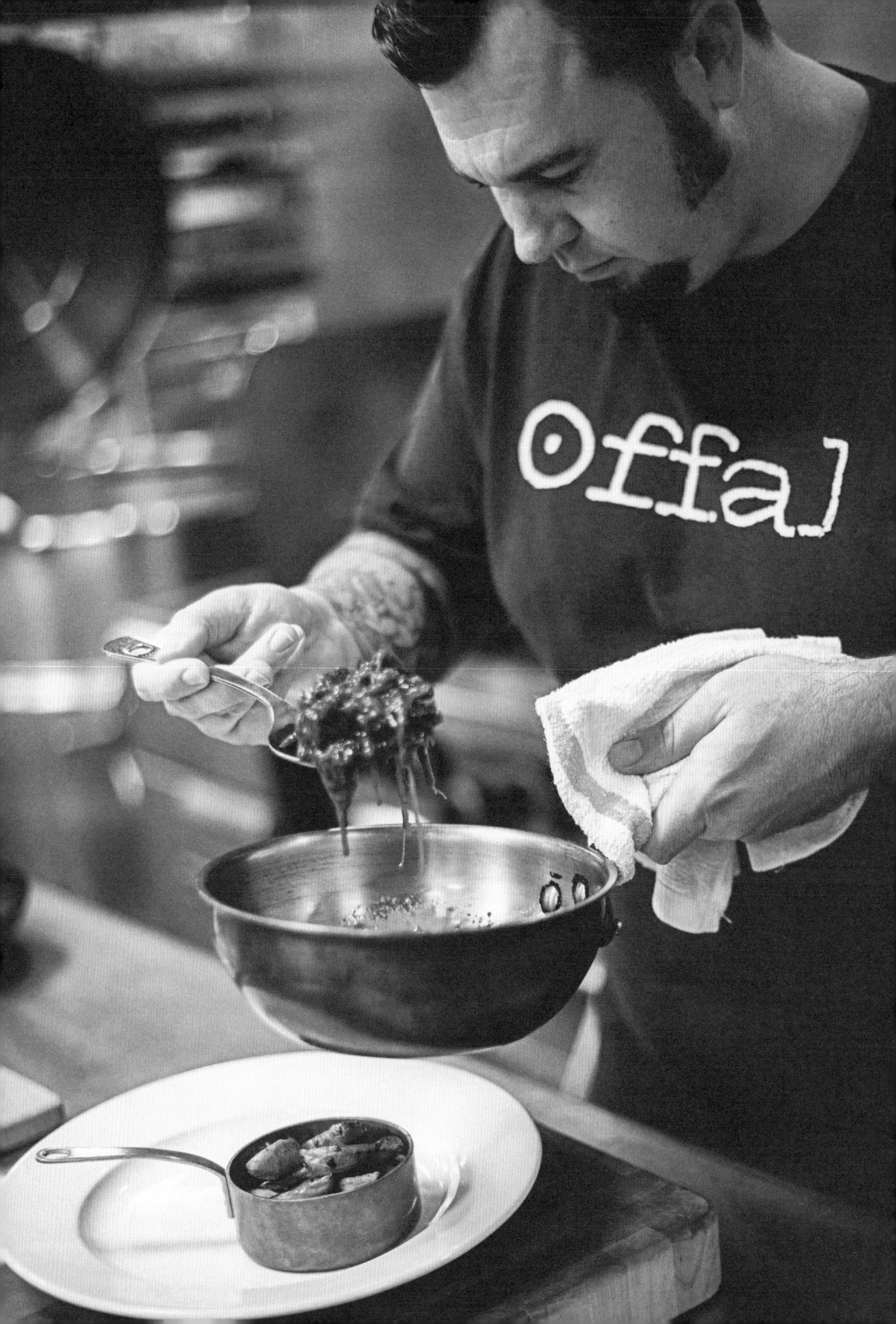
Offal

VLAAMSE STOOFKARBONADEN A LA ORSAY

Brian Siebenschuh, *Restaurant Orsay*

MAKES 8 TO 12 SERVINGS, DEPENDING ON HOW HUNGRY YOUR GUESTS ARE

10 pounds beef, any cut that one would use for a stew, cut into 2" chunks
1 handful fresh thyme sprigs
A few bay leaves
Canola oil
10 pounds yellow onions, cut into ½" dice
1 handful brown sugar
2 quarts Punk Monk Dubbel
2 quarts TCB Black Rye Ale
5 or 6 slices of good quality whole grain bread or pumpernickel
½ cup Dijon mustard
1 pound unsalted butter
Kosher salt
Black pepper
Cooked white rice or fingerling potatoes, to serve

Chef Siebenschuh says this recipe's title translates to "Flemish-style Braised Beef, made by an American guy that runs a French restaurant and has never been to Belgium." Recipes for this Flemish dish often emphasize using a quality beer as the sauce is built on the beer rather than on a meat-based stock or broth. A large quantity of two styles of beers and what the chef calls "an insane amount of onions" results in an incredibly deep, balanced, flavorful stew.

....

Preheat oven to 300°F.

Season beef aggressively with salt and pepper.

Break up the thyme sprigs into smaller pieces and tie the thyme and bay leaves up into a little pouch using cheese cloth and butcher twine (this way you don't have to go through and pick them out later).

Heat a nice thick film of oil over high heat in the bottom of your largest pot or pan. Brown the meat in batches, keeping an eye on your heat. You want to develop a nice brown fond in the bottom of the pan, which will later become part of the sauce, so don't let all those crispy bits that develop get burned up.

Once all the beef is nicely browned on all sides, remove it to a plate. Throw all the onions in the pan (assuming your pot or pan is large enough; if not, you'll have to improvise). Shake and stir the pan violently and, as the onions start to release their water, that nice brown fond on the bottom of the pan will release and coat the onions in goodness. Continue cooking at full blast, moving the onions around regularly, until the onions start to brown. Stir in the brown sugar and immediately add the beer, then bring to a simmer.

As soon as the beer is warmed through, combine the beef, beer/onion mixture, and your little satchel of thyme and bay in a pot or pan large enough to hold everything. Cover and cook in the oven for about an hour.

Remove the pan, uncover, and (I knows this sounds crazy) - spread the mustard on the slices of bread. Lay the bread, mustard side down, across the top of the stew. Cover and return to the oven for another hour, then check for doneness - you want the meat to be completely fork tender, and by this point the bread should have more or less dissolved into the sauce. Cook up to another hour or so, if necessary.

Once the beef is tender, remove the herb sachet, skim any fat that may be on top of the stew using a small ladle and discard. Allow to cool on the counter for an hour or two and then pour the entire batch through a large coarse strainer. Move the beef and onions to a container and put in the fridge to cool, then strain the sauce again through a fine strainer into a clean saucepot and return to the stovetop. Simmer over low heat until reduced by 25% - 50%. You only need enough sauce to nicely coat the meat – you're not looking to make soup here - but be careful of over-reducing, as you don't want your sauce to become too salty or intense.

Once the sauce is done, combine with the cooled beef and onion mixture and rest on the countertop until cool enough to handle, then shred the meat by hand (gloves are nice here). Refrigerate the whole shebang overnight.

To finish the dish the following day, reheat in a pot and slowly stir in a handful of cold, cubed butter to add a bit of richness to the sauce (or if you want to go nuts, use poached, cooled and diced bone marrow).

Serve with plain white rice (traditional), or pan-fried fingerling potatoes and crispy slivered garlic (new school).

UNDERDARK BEER CHILI

Alex *The Gourmet Aviator* Montañez

SERVES 4

2 pounds lean sirloin ground beef

2 packages Goya Sazon
(a seasoning blend found
in the Latino section of
most stores or online)

2 tablespoons cumin

2 tablespoons garlic, minced

1 teaspoon salt

1 large onion, diced

8 ounces sweet mini peppers,
diced

1 can diced tomatoes

1 bottle Underdark

1 lime, cut into wedges
(for serving)

Queso fresco, crumbled
(for serving)

This easy, speedy chili from food truck favorite Alex Montañez can be prepared with added black beans if you're looking for Latin flair or it can be adapted for a vegetarian audience by using a crumbled meat substitute. The bourbon-barrel aging of Underdark adds flavor and complexity to the mix, but you could also substitute with King Street Stout.

Brown the ground beef in a skillet over medium high heat. Add the Sazón seasoning, cumin, garlic, salt, onions and peppers. Stir it well and continue browning the meat for 2 more minutes. Add the diced tomatoes and about ½ bottle of beer and stir well. Bring to boil and simmer for about 20 minutes.

Add additional beer as desired.

To serve, garnish chili with a wedge of lime and sprinkle queso fresco on top.

BEER GROWLER CHICKEN SAISON

Tom Gray, *Moxie Kitchen + Cocktails*

SERVES 4

4 bone-in, skin-on chicken breasts
    (with rib)
2 teaspoons olive oil
1 medium white onion, peeled, cut
    into thin wedges
5 garlic cloves, peeled and
    smashed
Parsley, thyme and tarragon
    sprigs, tied together in a
    small bundle
12 ounces Session Saison
    (plus more for drinking)
2 teaspoons butter
1 lemon
1 teaspoon each parsley, dill,
    tarragon, lemon thyme,
    chopped
Salt and freshly ground
    black pepper
Whipped potatoes, to serve

Two-time James Beard Award nominee Chef Tom Gray offers up this savory take on chicken which utilizes Session Saison to deliver maximum flavor with an array of fresh herbs.

Preheat oven to 375°F.

Pat chicken breasts dry with a paper towel and heavily season with salt and freshly ground black pepper.

Using a non-stick or cast iron pan, sear chicken skin side down in olive oil over medium heat until golden brown and crispy. Remove chicken from pan and drain oil.

Place onion, garlic, bundled herbs and beer in pan, then add chicken, skin-side up. Bring to a boil, being careful not to let skin of the chicken get wet and lose its crispness.

Place entire pan in preheated oven to cook chicken through, about 15 minutes, depending on the size of the breasts. Remove from oven and set aside to allow chicken to rest.

Remove chicken from pan and strain vegetables from liquid. Discard vegetables, reserving liquid.

Place liquid back into the pan and bring to a simmer. Reduce to thicken over low heat. Stir in butter, lemon juice and half of the chopped herbs. Taste and adjust seasoning with salt and pepper if needed.

Serve by heating serving dish and pouring reduced sauce into bottom. Place chicken, skin-side up, on top of sauce and sprinkle with remaining herbs to garnish. Serve with creamy whipped potatoes.

JON BOAT CRAWFISH ETOUFFEE

Regina Heffington (aka Jax Brew Bitch), *The Silver Cow*

SERVES 4

1 stick unsalted butter
1 teaspoon salt
1 teaspoon black pepper
½ teaspoon cayenne pepper
    (add another ½ teaspoon
    if you prefer spicier)
1 teaspoon Cajun seasoning
1 bay leaf
1 onion, finely chopped
2 cloves garlic, finely chopped
1 stalk celery, finely chopped
1 tablespoon green onions,
    chopped, white and green
    parts separated
½ cup Jon Boat Coastal Ale
1 pound crawfish tail meat
Steamed rice, for serving
Gumbo filé, for garnishing
French bread, for serving
Green salad, for serving

Etouffee is a French word best described as "smothered," which comes from putting a tight lid on the top of this dish to keep the goodness inside. Regina shares this traditional family recipe for the Cajun/Creole dish and tells us that gumbo filé is a spicy herb made from dried and ground leaves of the sassafras tree. You can find it in most gourmet shops and online.

Melt butter in a pan then add salt, black pepper, cayenne pepper, Cajun seasoning and bay leaf.

Add onion, garlic, celery and white tips from green onions and sauté for 5 - 8 minutes. Add beer and bring to a simmer.

Add crawfish tail meat, stir well, cover and simmer on medium-low for 20 minutes, stirring occasionally. You may need to add a little more beer if etouffee gets too thick. If it's too thin, just add a ½ teaspoon of corn starch (or Gumbo filé) for thickening.

Serve the etouffee over steamed rice. Garnish with gumbo filé and green onions and accompany with French bread and a green salad.

KING STREET BBQ PORK BELLY WITH WAINWRIGHT CHEDDAR GRITS AND PICKLED MUSTARD SEEDS

Waylon Rivers, *Black Sheep Restaurant*

SERVES 6 TO 8

Roasted Pork Belly, sliced into
    2 to 3 ounce portions (see
    recipe below)
Canola oil
King Street Stout BBQ Sauce
    (see recipe below)
Wainwright Cheddar Grits
    (see recipe below)
Pickled Mustard Seeds
    (see recipe below)
Chives, to garnish

For Roasted Pork Belly:

4 cups of water
2 ounces kosher salt
2 ounces brown sugar
2 tablespoons molasses
1 tablespoon toasted coriander
    (optional)
1 tablespoon toasted mustard
    seeds (optional)
2 sprigs of thyme
1 teaspoon of whole black
    peppercorns
2 1/2 pounds pork belly

You can't miss the sexy, glittery slice of architecture gracing the wedge of Margaret and Oak these days. If you'd like a little sophisticated Black Sheep gorgeousness in the comfort of your own home, give these recipes a try. Rooftop dining is optional.

....

Preheat oven to 400°F.

Heat a small amount of oil in a saucepan over medium heat. Add sliced pork belly and sear on both sides until golden brown and crispy, about 2-3 minutes per side.

When the pork belly is done, pour BBQ sauce over the belly, adding just enough to cover the belly. Place pork belly in the oven and roast until the sauce starts to glaze onto the belly.

To serve, place the desired amount of Wainwright Cheddar Grits into a shallow bowl. Place BBQ pork belly on top of the grits and garnish with Pickled Mustard Seeds and sliced chives.

For roasted pork belly:

Heat water to a simmer in a large saucepan then add all remaining ingredients (except pork). Stir until ingredients are completely dissolved. Chill the brine before submersing the pork belly in it. Let belly brine for 12 hours.

Preheat oven to 400°F.

While oven is heating, remove pork belly from brine and pat dry with paper towels.

Place pork in a deep roasting pan. Cook for 30 minutes then baste with fat from the bottom of the pan and cook for 30 more minutes. Lower the temperature to 200°F and cook for another hour, basting every 30 minutes. Remove from the oven and let cool completely before slicing into 2 to 3 ounce portions.

For King Street Stout BBQ Sauce:

YIELDS 3 CUPS

2 tablespoons vegetable oil
1 medium onion, finely diced
3 cups Roma tomatoes, medium
    diced
8 ounces King Street Stout
¼ cup molasses
2 tablespoons Dijon mustard
⅓ cup apple cider vinegar
2 tablespoon dark brown sugar
1 tablespoon Worcestershire sauce
Kosher salt and freshly ground
    black pepper to taste

For Wainwright Cheddar Grits:

SERVES 6 TO 8

4 cups water or chicken stock
2 cups stone ground grits
4 cups heavy cream
½ pound of butter, cut into cubes
1 cup Wainwright cheddar or
    sharp white cheddar
Kosher salt and pepper to taste

For Pickled Mustard Seeds:

YIELDS 1 CUP

½ cup whole yellow mustard seeds
¾ cup water
¾ cup rice wine vinegar
¼ cup sugar
½ tablespoon of kosher salt

Make King Street Stout BBQ Sauce:

Heat oil in medium saucepan over medium heat until oil is just below starting to shimmer in the pan.

Add the onion and cook until lightly browned, about 7 to 8 minutes, stirring occasionally.

Stir in the tomatoes, beer, molasses, mustard, vinegar, brown sugar and Worcestershire sauce. Bring to a boil and then reduce to a simmer and cook until sauce is reduced to a medium-thin thickness, about 30 to 45 minutes, stirring occasionally. Season with salt and pepper to taste.

Transfer the sauce to a blender and puree until smooth. Store in the refrigerator until ready to use.

Make Wainwright cheddar grits:

In a large saucepan, heat water or chicken stock to a boil and add grits while stirring vigorously to prevent sticking to the bottom. Turn down to a simmer and cook for 1 to 1 ½ hours. Stir very often during the cooking process. When the grits are smooth and creamy add the cream, butter and cheese. Season with salt and pepper as desired and keep warm.

Pickle mustard seeds:

Combine all ingredients in a small heavy bottom sauce pan and bring to a low gentle simmer over low heat. Stir often until mustard seeds are plump and tender, about 45 minutes.

If seeds look like they are beginning to dry out add water as necessary to keep them barely submerged.

Cool off in the fridge when done. Drain off any excess liquid before serving.

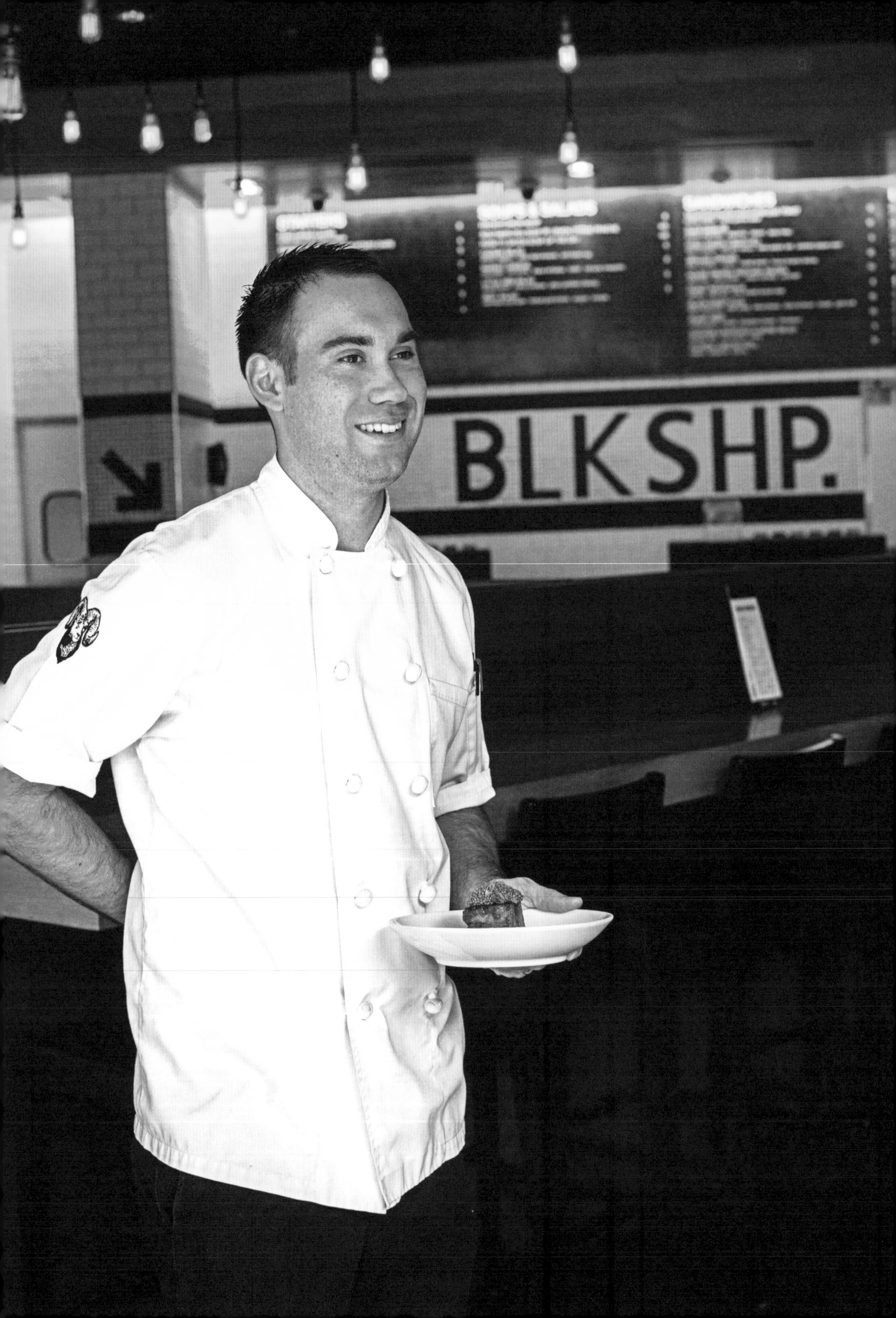
BLKSHP.

PUNKED-UP COTTAGE PIE

Laura Evans, *Laura Evans Photography*

SERVES 4-6

1- 12 ounce package firm
or extra firm tofu

2-3 cups Punk Monk, divided

½ cup soy sauce

2 pounds sweet potatoes

6 tablespoons olive oil, divided

1 large yellow onion, thinly sliced

2 turnips, peeled and diced

2 stalks celery, chopped

2 carrots, chopped

1 fennel bulb, sliced

2 cups Brussels sprouts, halved

2 tablespoons chopped flat-leaf
parsley

1 sprig fresh rosemary

1 - 14.5 ounce can vegetable broth

1-2 cups fresh spinach (or kale,
if desired)

¼ cup breadcrumbs (optional)

1 tablespoon melted butter for
breadcrumbs (if included)

There's no need to deny yourself the glorious pleasures of traditional cottage pie just because you're vegetarian. With this recipe, Laura shows us how to get all the savory, homespun goodness of this comfort food staple utilizing vegetables and Punk Monk. Scoop out a satisfying slab and put on your fuzzy socks!

Preheat oven to 400° F.

Remove tofu from package, pouring out any water in the package. Cut into 1/4" cubes and place in a bowl. Mix 1 cup beer and soy sauce, pour over tofu and let marinate for at least 30 minutes.

Pierce sweet potatoes with a fork and place on rimmed baking sheet lined with foil. Bake 30-45 minutes until tender. When cool enough to handle, peel off skin and mash.

Reduce oven to 350° F.

While tofu is marinating and sweet potatoes are baking, heat 2 tablespoons of olive oil in a large saucepan over medium heat. Add onion and sauté until translucent. Add turnips, celery, carrots, fennel, Brussels sprouts and parsley and mix well. Add rosemary, broth and 1 cup of beer, stir, cover and simmer until vegetables are tender, 15 to 20 minutes. Remove pan from heat. With a slotted spoon, move vegetables into a large bowl, being sure to keep cooking liquid in the pan. Salt and pepper vegetables to taste.

Pour tofu and marinating liquid into the pan. Simmer 10-15 minutes, stirring occasionally and adding beer and/or broth if needed. Use a slotted spoon to transfer tofu to a 1.5 quart casserole dish.

Place spinach or kale over tofu. Spread cooked vegetables on top of greens, then spread mashed sweet potatoes in an even layer on top. Sprinkle with breadcrumbs and drizzle with melted butter.

Bake at 350° F until bubbly then broil until lightly browned, about 3 to 5 minutes. Serve with a salad.

PEOPLE'S QUAIL AND KALE

Arielle Coutu, *Tapa That*

SERVES 2

4 tablespoons butter, divided
1 tablespoon oil
4 quail
1 shallot, cut in half lengthwise
    and thinly sliced, divided
8 cloves of garlic, thinly sliced,
    divided
1 tablespoon flour
¾ cup plus 1 tablespoon
    People's Pale Ale
⅓ cup milk
1 lemon
1 bunch curly kale
Salt
Chives, for garnishing

This is a recipe which allows you to produce an impressive restaurant-quality dish that is sure to wow an audience. Quail is available at specialty grocery stores and online, but you could easily substitute sautéed shrimp to fit nicely with the flavor profile. The kale can even stand on its own for a flavorful vegan option.

Preheat oven to 350° F.

Heat 1 tablespoon butter and 1 tablespoon oil in a heavy skillet and sear quail skin side down until it has a crispy, golden skin.

Remove quail from pan and place in baking dish skin side up.

In the same pan, heat another tablespoon of butter with a drop of oil. Add all but 1/3 of the shallot and garlic and sauté until they are translucent and starting to brown. Stir in the flour and let cook a minute or two before slowly adding 3/4 cup of the beer, stirring constantly.

Once the beer is incorporated and the liquid begins to thicken, stir in the milk, the juice of 1/2 the lemon and a pinch of salt. Pour sauce over quail and bake for 25-45 minutes (depending on your oven) or until meat reaches an internal temperature of 165° F.

While quail is roasting, add remaining butter, shallots and garlic to the pan and sauté until golden brown, about 5 to 10 minutes. Rip kale off of the thick woody stems and add to the pan with a pinch of salt. Cook until kale wilts but still retains its bright green color. Squeeze in the remaining lemon juice and pour in the remaining tablespoon of People's Pale Ale.

Arrange quail on top of kale then pour remaining braising liquid over top. Garnish with chives.

SHOTGUN SHACK BRAISED BONELESS BEEF SHORT RIBS

Fernando Silveria, *Catering by Liz*

SERVES 4

3 pounds boneless beef short ribs
5 tablespoons canola oil, divided
1 large carrot, diced
3 stalks celery, diced
1 small white onion, diced
1 tablespoon garlic, chopped
1 tablespoon shallot, chopped
1 ½ pints Shotgun Shack
    Black Rye Ale
1 ½ pints chicken stock
2 sprigs rosemary
1 spring sage
1 teaspoon thyme, chopped
Salt & pepper, to taste
Pappardelle or polenta, to serve

Short ribs are uniquely suited to be braised in beer. The meat gives itself over to the flavors, softens into unctuous morsels and pulls in the essence of the braising liquid beautifully. Here, Chef Silveria adds aromatic vegetables and herbs to the short ribs' braise for a rich, meaty entrée.

Preheat oven to 325°F.

Preheat a large Dutch oven over medium heat. The pot needs to accommodate all of the meat and allow it to be two thirds covered with the braising liquid.

Season the short ribs with salt and pepper. Add 2 tablespoons oil to Dutch oven and sear the meat on all sides until it's a dark caramel color. Achieving a dark caramel color is the most important step in the process! Once the beef is browned remove it to a plate.

Add a few more tablespoons of cooking oil to the pot then add the carrots and begin to cook. Add celery and onions and continue to cook for 3-5 minutes, and then add the garlic and shallots. Again you are looking to achieve a dark caramel color without burning the vegetables.

Pour the beer into the pot and scrape up all of the bits that have stuck to the bottom of the pan – this is the "fond" where much of the flavor will be. Let the beer simmer for 2-3 minutes then add the short ribs back to the pan. Cover meat two thirds of the way up with chicken stock and bring to a simmer. Nestle the rosemary and sage into the braising liquid and scatter the thyme over the meat.

When you have reached a simmer cover the pan and place it in the oven for two and a half hours. You should be able to insert a fork and remove it from the meat with no resistance.

Serve short ribs over pappardelle tossed with parsley and butter or polenta with cheddar.

THE PEOPLE'S BBQ TOFU BANH MI

Shana and Tim Massett, *Sun-Ray Cinema*

SERVES 4

16-ounce water-packed, extra
    firm tofu, drained and cut into
    ½" thick triangular wedges
4 hoagie rolls, toasted
Mayonnaise or vegan mayonnaise
    substitute, to taste
Fresh cilantro, to taste
Soy sauce, to taste
Sriracha, to taste

For tofu marinade:

16 ounces People's Pale Ale
1 teaspoon fresh ginger, grated
⅔ cup barbecue sauce
3 cloves garlic, minced
2 teaspoons – ⅛ cup "Fish" Sauce
    (see recipe below)

For pickled veggies:

⅓ cup brown rice vinegar
¼ teaspoon sugar
½ teaspoon salt
1 cup carrots, grated
1 cucumber, sliced thin

For "Fish" Sauce:

MAKES 2 ½ CUPS
(you may want to halve or
quarter this recipe it for
use in the banh mi
recipe)

¼ cup water
2 ½ cups honey
    (use sugar to
    make it vegan!)
¼ cup pineapple juice
2 tablespoons soy sauce
½ tablespoon salt
⅛ teaspoon ground ginger

Banh Mi are wildly popular Vietnamese sandwiches. The phrase itself means "bread", specifically the thin-crusted airy single-serve baguette, which is the most common bread in the region. They are most often stuffed with crispy pickled vegetables, meats and fish sauce. Here, the Massetts put a vegan spin on the Banh Mi with gingery barbecue People's Pale marinated tofu and a vegetarian "fish" sauce.

....

Marinate the tofu:

Whisk marinade ingredients in a large shallow pan and let tofu soak for at least one hour or overnight for good measure.

Pickle the veggies:

Mix vinegar, sugar and salt until dissolved then add the carrots and cucumbers to the mixture.

Refrigerate for at least 30 minutes.

Cook the tofu:

Remove tofu from marinate and grill in a Panini press or pan fry on medium heat with a heavy weight on top. The tofu should end up golden brown on the outside and light and chewy inside.

Assemble the banh mi:

Smear the hoagie rolls with mayonnaise and add two wedges of tofu, soy sauce, pickled veggies, cilantro and sriracha to taste. Wrap in waxed paper with a rubber band for maximum authenticity.

Make the "Fish" Sauce:

Stir all ingredients together and let sit for at least 30 minutes. Lasts in refrigerator up to two weeks.

SWORDFISH, KALE AND SOUR CREAM MASHED POTATOES WITH JON BOAT BEURRE BLANC

Howard Kirk, *13 Gypsies*

SERVES 1, WITH EXTRA POTATOES

Howard Kirk shares these individual recipes to create a full meal which will impress even the most sophisticated foodie. Simple, honest ingredients are united with a Jon Boat Beurre Blanc for a rich and satisfying offering.

....

For Jon Boat Beurre Blanc:

1 shallot, peeled and minced
½ – 12 ounce can Jon Boat Coastal Ale
Juice of 1 fresh-squeezed lemon
6 black peppercorns
5 tablespoons cold butter, divided into 5 equal parts
1 teaspoon heavy cream, room temperature (optional)
½ teaspoon Dijon mustard
Salt and white pepper, to taste

For Sour Cream Mashed Potatoes:

5 large potatoes, peeled and cut into chunks
1 stick butter, melted
¾ cup sour cream, room temperature
½ heavy cream, warmed
Sea salt and white pepper

Sauteed Kale

Fresh kale, stems removed
Extra virgin olive oil
Garlic, peeled and thinly sliced
Sea salt and black pepper

Make Jon Boat beurre blanc:

In a small saucepan combine the shallots, beer, lemon juice, and black peppercorns. Reduce until the saucepan is almost dry. Pull off the heat and allow it to sit for 1 minute. Whisk in the COLD butter, one pat at a time. Season with salt and white pepper if needed.

Strain into a small bowl to remove the shallots and peppercorns. This sauce can be temperamental; adding the optional heavy cream in BEFORE the first pat of butter will help with stability. If using the heavy cream, do not give the pan a one minute rest period.

Stir the Dijon mustard into the beurre blanc.

Make sour cream mashed potatoes:

Boil the potatoes in salted water until fork tender. Strain. Put strained potatoes into a large bowl. Add the melted butter and begin to mash with a hand held potato masher or hand mixer if you like them extra smooth. Add the sour cream and continue to mash. While mashing, add warm cream a little at a time until your mashed potatoes are at the consistency you like. Add white pepper and more salt (if needed) to your liking. Remember to use melted butter, room temperature sour cream, and warm milk. You do not want to add any cold ingredients to your warm potatoes.

Saute kale:

Place pan over low heat. Pour enough olive oil in the pan to eventually coat the kale. Place the garlic slices in the olive oil and allow to steep in the oil for 1 to 2 minutes. Turn heat up to medium-high. When garlic begins to dance in the oil, toss in the raw kale and season with salt and pepper. Begin to turn and move the kale in the pan with a pair of tongs until slightly wilted.

Swordfish

Extra virgin olive oil
Swordfish fillet
Sea salt and black pepper

Make swordfish:

Place a sauté pan on high heat with olive oil. Season both sides of the swordfish with salt and pepper. Just as the oil in the pan begins to smoke, place the swordfish in the pan. Do not shake or move the pan. Allow the fish to cook for 2 1/2 to 4 minutes then carefully turn the fillet over using a fish slice or a spatula. Cook on this side for another 2 1/2 to 4 minutes. The 2 1/2 to 4 minutes cooking time in the recipe depends on the thickness of the fillet and how well done you like your fish.

Assemble dish:

To assemble, place a generous large scoop of mashed potatoes down on the place first. Using tongs, place the desired amount of kale on top of the potatoes lightly. Do not push down on the potatoes. Using a spatula or fish slice and a clean hand, gently place the swordfish on top of the kale. Spoon John Boat Beurre Blanc on top.

CHINESE PORK BELLY STEW

Dennis Chang, *Blue Bamboo*

SERVES 4

For marinade:

4 tablespoons soy sauce
½ teaspoon Chinese five-spice
    powder
2 pounds pork belly, cut into
    2-inch pieces

For stew:

3 tablespoons vegetable oil
1 cup broth of choice
1 cup Jon Boat Coastal Ale
4 tablespoons soy sauce
2 tablespoons hoisin sauce
¼ cup brown sugar
6 quarter-sized slices ginger,
    lightly crushed
6 green onion sprigs
2 sliced carrots
1 small onion, cut into 6 wedges
8 ounces red potatoes, cut into
    1-inch pieces
Cooked white rice, for serving

It's an obvious fact that you can't go wrong with pork belly and beer. In this dish, Chef Chang goes beyond those winning basics adding complex Asian flavors and hearty vegetables. It all adds up to a stew that is sure to satisfy.

Combine marinade ingredients in a bowl. Add pork, stirring to coat. Cover, refrigerate and marinate overnight.

Place a wok over high heat until hot. Add oil, swirling to coat sides. Add a batch of pork and cook, turning, until browned on all sides, about 5 minutes. Remove pork and transfer to a heavy-bottomed pot. Repeat with remaining pork.

Add the broth, beer, soy sauce, hoisin sauce, brown sugar and ginger to the pot with the pork and pour in enough water to cover. Bring to a boil. Reduce the heat to a medium low, cover and simmer gently until the meat is tender, about 1 hour.

Tuck the green onions, carrots, onion and potatoes into the cooking liquid and continue to cook, covered, until the vegetables are soft and the meat is fork-tender, about 30 minutes. Serve over rice.

PIMENTO CHEESE TWICE-BAKED POTATOES WITH BEER CARAMELIZED ONIONS

Cari Sánchez-Potter, *Intuition Ale Works*

**SERVES 4 AS A SIDE DISH
2 AS AN ENTRÉE**

2 large russet potatoes
Olive oil
8 tablespoons Riverside Red
   Pimento Cheese (p. 240)
2 tablespoons chives, chopped
   (plus more to garnish)
4 tablespoons Dragonglass
   Caramelized Onions
2 strips bacon, fried and crumbled
   (optional)
Salt and pepper

The stuffed baked potato is an endlessly adaptable item which works well in an array of menu situations. Small or half potatoes can be used as a side dish or heftier potatoes can be presented as a full meal. In this recipe, Cari shares the blend of creamy Riverside Red Pimento Cheese and Beer Caramelized Onions to create a potato dish that will be supremely satisfying. Omit the bacon for a handy vegetarian option.

Preheat oven to 450°F.

Scrub the potatoes clean. Rub the outside of the potatoes with olive oil and place directly on the middle rack of your oven. Roast for 1 hour, or until a knife inserted into the center of the potato meets no resistance.

Remove potatoes from oven and allow to cool just until you're able to handle them. Maintain oven temperature at 450°F.

Cut a small slice off the ends of the potatoes, then cut the potatoes in half crosswise, so each half can stand up on end like a bowl.

Using a teaspoon, scoop out the insides of the potatoes, leaving a shell and being careful not to break through the bottom. Place the scooped potato insides in a medium bowl. Season the potato shells with salt and pepper on the inside.

Add about 3 or 4 tablespoons pimento cheese per potato to the potato innards (depending on the consistency you like) and mash everything together well with a fork until smooth and creamy. Stir in about a tablespoon of chives per potato. Season potato filling to taste with salt and pepper.

Stuff potato shells with pimento cheese potato filling, being careful not to break the shells.

Lightly oil the bottom of a baking dish that's just big enough to hold the stuffed potatoes. Stand the stuffed potatoes in the baking dish and bake in preheated oven for about 15 minutes, or until the filling is heated through.

Top each stuffed potato with a spoonful of beer caramelized onions and a sprinkling of chives.

RIVERSIDE RED PIMENTO CHEESE

MAKES 4 CUPS

8 ounces extra sharp orange
    cheddar cheese, grated
8 ounces Vermont sharp-white
    cheddar cheese, grated
2 cloves garlic, grated
¼ cup onion, grated
1 teaspoon Worcestershire sauce
½ to 1 cup Riverside Red
1 teaspoon dry mustard
1 – 7-ounce jar diced pimento
    peppers, drained
1/2 cup mayonnaise
Several splashes of hot sauce
Cayenne pepper, to taste
Salt and freshly ground pepper,
    to taste

The aggressively hoppy flavor of Riverside Red plays very nicely with the sharp cheddar cheeses and pimento peppers in this recipe to produce a spreadable delight which will fulfill all your spreading and topping needs. Don't skip the hot sauce or cayenne here if you're concerned, simply give it a taste as you process the spread and add it a little at a time.

Place all ingredients in a food processor and pulse until lightly blended. Refrigerate overnight. (The pimento cheese will seem very loose but will firm up overnight in the fridge.)

DRAGONGLASS CARAMELIZED ONIONS

MAKES 2 CUPS

1 tablespoon canola oil
3 tablespoons unsalted butter
6 large white onions, thinly sliced
2 tablespoons light brown sugar
2 tablespoons white wine vinegar
1 cup Dragonglass
Salt and freshly ground black
    pepper

Besides being put to use in twice-baked potatoes or used to top burgers, you could also consider using these to top grilled sausages, as a nice companion for steak, a goat cheese/bruschetta situation or as an accompaniment for any flavor of roast beast.

Heat the canola oil and butter in a large heavy-bottomed sauté pan or Dutch oven over medium high heat. Add the sliced onions and cook, stirring occasionally, for 10 minutes until onions are slightly softened. (I know it seems like a LOT of onions but they will cook down substantially!) Add the brown sugar, vinegar, salt and pepper and continue to cook, stirring occasionally, another 15 minutes or until the onions start to develop a golden color.

Stir in beer, bring to a boil, reduce heat to medium and simmer the onions uncovered for 30-35 minutes until onions are golden and all liquid has evaporated. Taste for seasoning.

TRIPEL THAI CURRY WITH SHRIMP

Jessie and Kevin O'Brien, *Intuition Ale Works*

SERVES 2 TO 4

For curry paste:

2 inch piece of fresh ginger,
   peeled and roughly
   chopped
3 cloves of garlic, roughly chopped
1 shallot, roughly chopped
3 tablespoons lemongrass paste or
   chopped lemongrass stalk
1 dried red bird's eye chili,
   rehydrated (optional)
1 tablespoon cayenne pepper
2 teaspoons turmeric
1 teaspoons cinnamon
½ teaspoon star anise
½ teaspoon salt

For curry:

1 large white onion, sliced
2 red bell peppers, sliced
1 cup carrots, chopped
1 ¼ cup Triad Tripel
1 - 12 ounce can coconut milk
2 tablespoons brown sugar
1 tablespoon curry paste
2 tablespoons lime juice
1 pound shrimp, peeled and
   deveined
Salt, to taste
Noodles or rice, for serving

The spice, fruit and malt notes in Triad Tripel are a natural fit with this Thai-inspired curry. The heat level can be easily adjusted by how much chili and spice you put in the paste and how much paste you put in the curry.

....

Make curry paste:

Combine all ingredients in a food processor and blend into a fine paste. The recipe makes 1/2 cup of paste.

Make curry:

In a large skillet, sauté the onion, bell pepper and carrot for 8 to 10 minutes until the onions are soft. Add one cup of the Tripel to the pan and then slowly stir in the coconut milk, breaking up any clumps.

Stir in the brown sugar, curry paste and lime juice. When adding the curry paste, you can begin with ½ a tablespoon and keep adding more until you reach your preferred level of spiciness. Bring the curry to a gentle boil and add the shrimp.

Continue cooking, stirring occasionally, for 15 minutes. Add the remaining ¼ cup of Tripel and cook for 2 to 4 more minutes until the beer reduces into the sauce.

Season to taste with salt, and serve over noodles or rice.

PORCINI DUSTED CERVENA VENISON WITH CELERIAC PUREE, JUNIPER BRAISED CABBAGE, CRISP GARLIC HARICOT VERTS AND KING STREET STOUT DEMI-GLACE

Jamey Evoniuk, *The Chef's Garden* and *Café at The Cummer*

For Venison:

Dried porcini mushrooms,
    or a blend of dried wild
    mushrooms
2 pounds Denver leg cut venison,
    portioned into four
    8-ounce portions
Kosher salt and fresh cracked
pepper
Olive oil

For Celeriac Puree:

1 cup heavy cream
1 pound celeriac, cleaned and cut
    into 1 inch cubes
1 pound Idaho potatoes, peeled
    and quartered
½ pound unsalted butter, melted
Salt and pepper

For Juniper Braised Cabbage:

1 cup pecan wood smoked bacon,
    diced (optional)
1 Vidalia or other sweet onion,
    julienned
1 fennel bulb, julienned
1 head purple cabbage, shredded
1 cup apple cider vinegar
1 Honeycrisp apple, peeled
    and diced
⅔ cup light brown sugar
8 lightly toasted juniper berries,
    wrapped in cheesecloth
3 sprigs thyme
Salt and pepper

This recipe is extremely impressive, both in preparation and in the finished dish. Don't be intimidated by unfamiliar terms, just see the notes for definition and sourcing and then Chef Jamey will walk you right through the preparation.

....

Make venison:

Pulse dried mushrooms in a food processor until mushrooms resemble sawdust (do not process so finely that they are reduced to a powder).

Lightly coat venison with olive oil, season with salt and pepper and dredge in mushroom dust.

Sear on all sides on medium high heat to an internal temperature of 125. Venison is very lean and overcooking will leave it tough and gamey. Let the meat rest for 5-10 minutes then slice into ¼ inch medallions.

Make celeriac puree:

Bring cream to as simmer in a small sauce pot over medium heat. Add the celeriac and cook until fork tender. Remove from heat, allow to cool slightly and then puree in a blender, being careful not to over fill blender as hot liquid (steam) will expand. Boil potatoes in lightly salted water till tender.

Rice the potatoes over the melted butter and incorporate the celeriac puree till smooth. (Note: Ricing is the process of squeezing potatoes through a ricing mechanism either specially made for it or by passing them through a food mill.)

Season to taste with salt and pepper.

Make juniper braised cabbage:

In a skillet over medium heat, sweat the bacon and onions. Add fennel and cabbage and sauté for 2 to 3 minutes. Add remaining ingredients then lower the temperature and braise, covered, for 30 minutes or until the cabbage is tender but not completely broken down.

For King Street Demi Glace:

4 cups King Street stout
4 cups demi glace

For assembling dish:

1 pound snipped haricot verts,
    blanched but still crisp
Celeriac chips, for garnishing

Make King Street demi-glace:

Reduce beer by half in a saucepan and add demi-glace. Reduce by half again and strain through a fine sieve. Season to taste with salt and pepper. The reduction should hold when drizzled on a plate. If it is still too loose reduce until a syrup texture is achieved.

Assemble dish:

Put celeriac puree in a piping bag fitted with a star tip and pipe from top left of the plate to the center in an elevated clockwise fashion.

Fan venison medallions in front of the piped puree. Place haricots to the right of the venison, pointed tips up, then cover the base with the cabbage. Spoon the sauce at the base of the meat and top with celeriac chips.

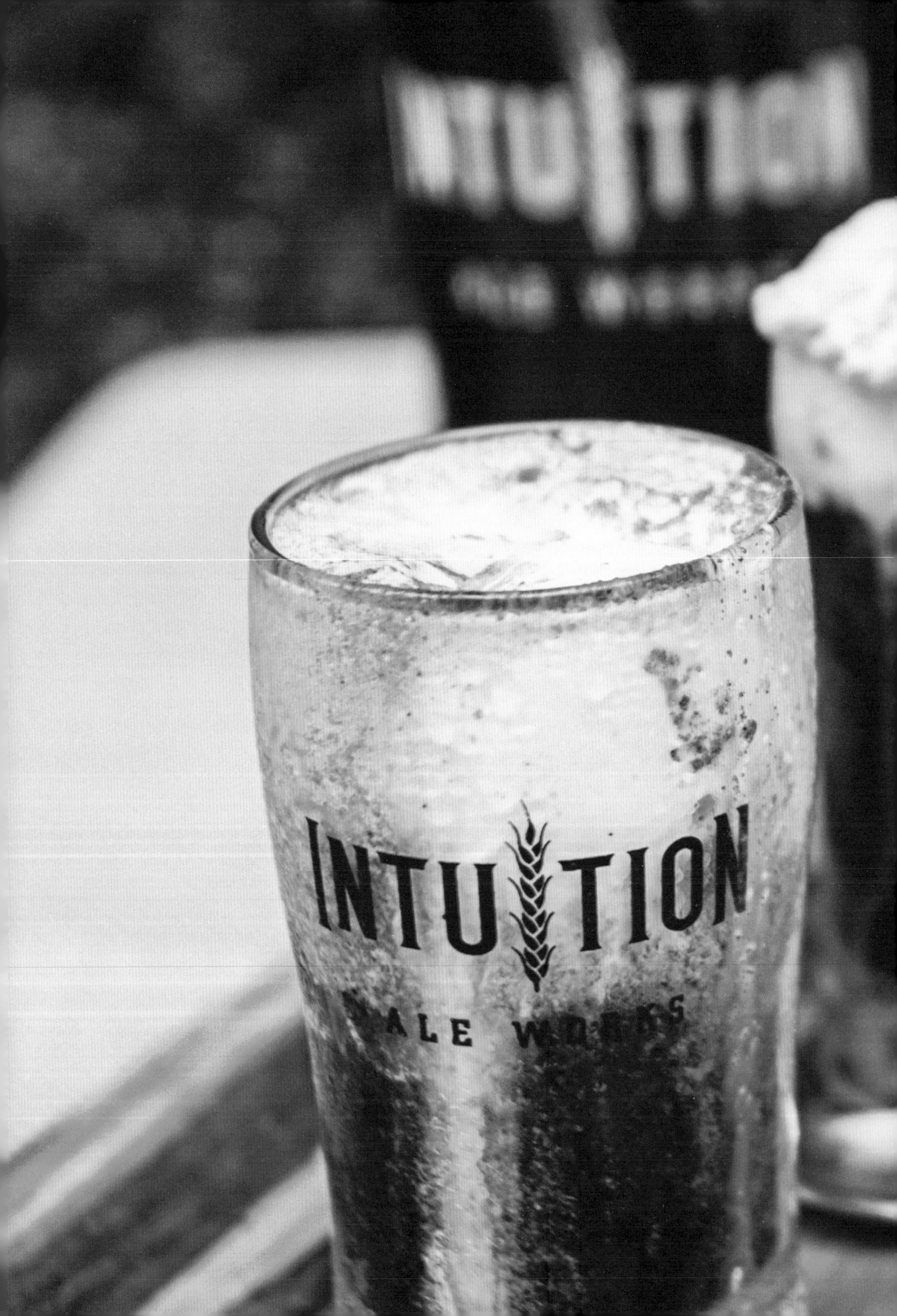
INTUITION

DESSERTS

TRUCK STOP STOUT PECAN PIE BARS WITH BACON MAPLE GLAZE

Sarah Hall, *Second Harvest North Florida*

SERVES 12

Cooking spray
2 cups 100% whole wheat flour
1 cup brown sugar
½ cup chopped pecans
¾ teaspoon salt
¼ teaspoon baking soda
2 teaspoons cinnamon
8 tablespoons butter, melted
¾ cup Truck Stop Stout
2 large eggs
2 teaspoons vanilla

For Bacon Maple Glaze:

¼ cup salted butter
½ cup pure maple syrup
¼ cup brown sugar
¼ cup heavy cream
6 slices thick-cut bacon, cooked
   until crispy and crumbled
½ cup chopped pecans

Second Harvest Food Bank had a staff-judged full-on food fight to determine which recipe would represent them in the cookbook. Sarah's delectable Pecan Pie Bars won the day, but the other two entries were so good, we included them all.

....

Preheat oven to 350°F.

Lightly spray a 9x13 baking dish with cooking spray to prevent sticking. In a mixing bowl, combine flour, brown sugar, pecans, salt, baking soda and cinnamon.

Add in the melted butter, beer, eggs and vanilla and mix until combined. The mixture will be the consistency of brownie batter.

Pour the mixture into your 9 x 13 pan and bake for 20 minutes. While the first layer is baking, assemble the glaze.

Make the glaze:

Melt butter in a saucepan then add maple syrup, brown sugar and heavy cream. Bring the mixture to a boil, stirring constantly. Boil at medium heat for about 1 1/2 minutes. Remove from heat and let it cool for about five minutes.

When your pan comes out of the oven, take a skewer or knife and poke about 10- 15 holes in the bars.

Finish the bars:

Once the glaze has cooled, pour on top of the bars and spread with the back of a spoon. Sprinkle the entire pan with chopped pecans and bacon crumbles and cut into squares.

JON BOAT STRAWBERRY SHORTCAKE

Michael Bump, *Restaurant Orsay*

1 quart strawberries, washed and
    cut into quarters
Jon Boat Syrup
    (see recipe below)
Jon Boat Pound Cake
    (see recipe below)
Jon Boat Whipped Cream
    (see recipe below)

Jon Boat Pound Cake

¾ pound butter, at room
    temperature
3 cups sugar
5 eggs
2 teaspoons vanilla extract
3 cups all-purpose flour
1 teaspoons salt
1 cup Jon Boat

Jon Boat Syrup

1 cup Jon Boat
½ vanilla bean
Zest of half a lemon, cut into large
    strips
1 ½ cups sugar

Jon Boat Whipped Cream

2 cups heavy cream
½ vanilla bean
¼ cup honey
2 tablespoons Jon Boat

Crisp, refreshing Jon Boat golden ale is the foundation for this classic dessert. Fresh strawberries, Jon Boat butter pound cake and whipped cream are topped with a lemony vanilla Jon Boat syrup for a serious wow-factor finish. Michael suggests serving any leftover syrup over ice cream.

....

For Jon Boat Syrup:

Place all ingredients in a sauce pan and bring to a boil. Simmer until syrup has lost about ¼ of its volume.

Strain and reserve.

For Jon Boat Pound Cake:

Preheat oven to 350°F. Spray two loaf pans liberally with pan spray.

In a stand mixer, cream butter then add sugar one cup at a time until incorporated into butter. Add vanilla, salt and eggs one at a time until incorporated. Add flour one cup at a time. When flour is incorporated mix in the beer until combined.

Divide batter between the two loaf pans and bake for about an hour or until toothpick inserted in center of cakes comes out clean. Cool loaves then wrap tightly with cellophane until ready to serve.

For Jon Boat Whipped Cream:

Place all ingredients in a stand mixer and whip to stiff peaks.

To assemble:

Pour ½ the Jon Boat Syrup over the berries and stir to coat well. Set aside.

Place two slices of Jon Boat Pound Cake on a plate and spoon some of the berries over the cake. Top with a scoop of whipped cream. (For an added bonus, place the slices of cake in a sauté pan with a little butter and lightly cook them to get a little color.)

PEOPLE'S PALE ALE ORANGE CARAMEL CUPCAKES WITH VANILLA BEAN ALE FROSTING AND CRYSTALLIZED GINGER

Katie Riehm, *Sweet Theory Baking Co.*

YIELDS 1 DOZEN CUPCAKES

2 cups all-purpose flour
1 cup sugar
1 ½ teaspoon baking soda
½ teaspoon sea salt
¼ teaspoon ground ginger
¼ teaspoon ground cardamom
Pinch ground cloves
¾ cup People's Pale Ale
½ cup Pale Ale Orange Caramel
    (see recipe below)
½ cup oil (we use organic
    coconut oil)
3 teaspoons vanilla extract
1 tablespoon apple cider vinegar
Vanilla Bean Ale Frosting
    (see recipe below)
Crystallized ginger, finely chopped
    (for garnish)
Orange zest (for garnish)

These lightly spiced cupcakes with fresh citrus beautifully compliment the crisp, hoppy notes of People's Pale Ale. What really puts these cupcakes over the edge is spooning the additional ale and orange spiked caramel over the cupcakes while they're still warm. You will have extra caramel left over, so be sure to pour it over ice cream, dip with sliced apples, or just eat it by the spoonful like we do.

....

Preheat the oven to 350. Line a cupcake pan with 12 cupcake liners.

In a medium bowl, sift together the flour, sugar, baking soda, salt, ginger, cardamom and cloves. Whisk to combine.

In another medium bowl, whisk together ale, caramel, oil, vanilla extract and apple cider vinegar.

Add the dry ingredients to the wet in two batches, whisking until just combined. DO NOT OVERMIX! You should have a thick batter.

Fill the cupcake liners ¾ of the way full (about ¼ cup batter), and bake for 17-20 minutes. The cupcakes should be golden brown and an inserted toothpick should come out clean.

While the cupcakes are still warm, prick several times with a toothpick and spoon about a tablespoon of caramel over the cake, working it in gently to soak into the cake.

When the cupcakes are cool, hand frost or pipe with Vanilla Bean Ale Frosting and top with extra caramel, then garnish with finely chopped crystallized ginger and fresh orange zest.

Pale Ale Orange Caramel

1 ½ cups People's Pale Ale
2 teaspoons orange zest
¼ cup rice or almond milk
6 tablespoons cornstarch
1 ½ cups coconut sugar
        or brown sugar
1 - 13 ounce can full fat
        coconut milk
1 tablespoon vanilla extract
½ teaspoon sea salt

Vanilla Bean Ale Frosting

1 ½ cups non-hydrogenated
        shortening
1 vanilla bean, split lengthwise,
        beans removed
3 cups powdered sugar, sifted
2 teaspoons vanilla extract
3 tablespoons People's Pale Ale

For Pale Ale Orange Caramel:

In a medium saucepan, combine ale and orange zest and heat on high at a rolling boil, whisking occasionally, until it reduces to roughly one cup, about 8-10 minutes.

Meanwhile, combine rice milk and cornstarch (we put ours in a blender) until no clumps of cornstarch remain to make a slurry.

Once the ale/zest mixture reduces, whisk in sugar and coconut milk. When it returns to a boil, whisk in the rice milk/cornstarch slurry, continue to whisk until the caramel is thick (it should coat the back of a spoon).

Remove from heat, and whisk in vanilla extract and sea salt.

For Vanilla Bean Ale Frosting:

Using a stand or hand mixer, beat the shortening and vanilla bean until fluffy and smooth.

In one cup increments, add in powdered sugar with 1 tablespoon pale ale, and beat until combined and fluffy. Add in vanilla extract and the rest of the beer, and beat for an additional 3-4 minutes.

STOUT POACHED PEARS

Chef Dennis Chang, *Blue Bamboo*

SERVES 4

1 quart growler King Street Stout
4 pears, peeled, cored, and halved
2 cups sugar
Ginger, orange peel, star anise,
    and cinnamon (optional)
Ice cream and crisp cookies,
    for serving

Three basic ingredients merge with warm spices to produce a dessert sure to please. Chef Chang uses Asian pears but any variety will produce excellent results.

The day before you plan to serve the pears, combine stout, pears, and sugar in a large saucepan and bring to a simmer.

Add your choice of spices and simmer for 20 minutes, checking with a knife for doneness. Let pears sit in liquid overnight. The next day, cut the pears and serve with your choice of ice cream and a crisp cookie.

NEARLY FAMOUS TRUCK STOP COOKIES

Gary Warren, *Mug Club #53*

½ **pound bacon, cut into julienne**
    slices
1 **cup Truck Stop Stout**
2 **medium eggs, roughly at room**
    temperature (put them
    in a bowl of warm water
    for a few minutes)
2 **sticks salted butter**
¼ **teaspoon table salt**
1 **teaspoon baking soda**
¼ **cup light brown sugar**
¼ **cup granulated sugar**
1 **teaspoon pure vanilla extract**
3 ¼ **cups all-purpose flour**
    + ¾ cup, reserved
1 **cup pecans**
1 **cup semi-sweet chocolate chips**
Sea salt, for finish before baking

Cupcakes, cake pops, quinoa, spelt, no-carb, copyrighted pastries, fusion tacos... we've all seen food fads come and go. Bacon is often lumped into the fad list, but there's historical proof that humanity would have died out and Revolutionary War pants would have been even more ill-fitting without bacon. True story. Here are bacon beer chocolate chip cookies by our good buddy, Gary. If the zombiepocalypse happens, we're with him.

Fry bacon to crispy or just a very little bit shy of crispy. Reserve bacon and drain off drippings. Place bacon and drippings in the refrigerator while you're doing the next step.

Add butter, salt, baking soda, sugars and vanilla to a stand mixer and mix on low speed for one minute.

Add beer and eggs, one at a time, to mixer while mixing on medium speed for another minute. Then mix on high for 4 minutes.

With the mixer off, add the first measure of flour. Mix at medium speed for 2 1/2 minutes. Check the consistency of the dough mixture – if it is too wet, add flour a tablespoon at a time and incorporate until cookie dough consistency is achieved.

Instead of chopping the pecans, break them up with your hands, they do not need to be precisely the same size. Taste a little bacon with a chocolate chip, nobody's watching. If they are, share.

Set the mixer to low and incorporate first the pecans, grab the bacon from the fridge and put in what looks right, nibble on the rest, and then finally incorporate the chocolate chips. Stop as soon as they're mixed in, don't over mix as your chocolate could begin to melt.

Optional step: Refrigerate the dough overnight. Not mandatory, but the cookies will rise better if the dough is cold.

Preheat oven to 350°F.

Coat cookie sheet with nonstick cooking spray or use parchment paper on top of your cookie sheet.

With a tablespoon dip out roughly the same size cookies and shape into small mounds or dollops on the cookie sheet. Leave a little room between cookies. If you want to be fancy, you can put a piece of bacon on top of each one. Sprinkle a very little bit of sea salt on each cookie. Don't worry about absolute uniformity, but make the cookies roughly the same size so that they'll all bake properly by the time you take them out.

Bake for approximately 9 minutes. You're shooting for them to be a bit crispy when they're cooled. If you bake them to where they are fully crispy when you take them out of the oven, they'll be dry when they cool. Every oven is different, so watch your cookies to get them right. (Reminder: if you use a dark cookie pan, reduce your baking temps accordingly).

Options:

You can use bacon grease instead of butter.

You can make variations using white chocolate chips, milk chocolate chips or a mix as variations. Even butterscotch chips.

Omit the salt if you want them to be more healthy. Wait, what?

SANCHEZ-PORTER STICKY TOFFEE PUDDING

Scott Schwartz, *29 South*

MAKES 8 PUDDING CAKES

Pudding cakes

1 ¼ cups whole dates, pitted, cut
    crosswise into ¼-inch
    slices, divided
½ teaspoon baking soda
1 ¼ cups unbleached all-purpose
    flour
½ teaspoon baking powder
½ teaspoon salt
¾ cup packed brown sugar
    (5 ¼ ounces), light or dark
¾ cup warm porter
large eggs
1 ½ teaspoons vanilla extract
4 tablespoons unsalted butter
    (1/2 stick), melted

Toffee sauce

8 tablespoons unsalted butter
    (1 stick)
1 cup packed brown sugar
    (7 ounces), light or dark
⅔ cup heavy cream
1 tablespoon rum
½ teaspoon juice from 1 lemon
Crème Anglaise or vanilla ice
    cream, for serving

For the toffee sauce:

Sanchez-Porter is a rare brew known by many, possessed by few but loved by all. If you can't get your hands on it, try this with Lowdown Porter. The rich flavor profile combines with dates and brown sugar for a decadent, sticky delight.

For the pudding cakes:

Adjust oven rack to middle position and heat oven to 350°F.

Grease and flour eight 4-ounce ramekins and line bottom of each with a round of parchment paper cut to fit. Set prepared ramekins in large roasting pan lined with a clean dish towel. Bring kettle or large saucepan of water to boil over high heat.

Combine half of dates with water and baking soda in glass measuring cup (dates should be submerged beneath water) and soak for 5 minutes. Drain dates, reserving liquid, and transfer to a medium bowl. Whisk flour, baking powder, and salt together in another medium bowl.

Process remaining dates and brown sugar in food processor until just blended, about five 1-second pulses. Add reserved soaking liquid, beer, eggs and vanilla and process until smooth, about 5 seconds. With food processor running, pour melted butter through feed tube in a steady stream. Transfer this mixture to bowl with softened dates.

Gently stir dry mixture into wet mixture until just combined and date pieces are evenly dispersed. Distribute batter evenly among prepared ramekins. Fill roasting pan with enough boiling water to come halfway up sides of ramekins, making sure not to splash water into ramekins. Cover pan tightly with aluminum foil, crimping edges to seal.

Bake pudding cakes until puffed and small holes appear on surface, about 40 minutes. Immediately remove ramekins from water bath and cool on wire rack for 10 minutes.

Meanwhile, melt butter in medium saucepan over medium heat. Whisk in brown sugar until smooth. Continue to cook, stirring occasionally, until sugar is dissolved and mixture looks puffy, 3 to 4 minutes.

Slowly pour in cream and rum, whisk just to combine, reduce heat and simmer until frothy, about 3 minutes. Remove from heat and stir in lemon juice.

To serve, invert each ramekin onto plate or shallow bowl, remove ramekin, and peel off parchment paper lining. Divide toffee sauce evenly among cakes and serve immediately, accompanied by crème anglaise or vanilla ice cream.

KING STREET STOUT MACADAMIA NUT AND CARAMEL ICE CREAM

Ian Lynch, *Ovinte*

MAKES ABOUT 1 QUART

3 cups heavy whipping cream
1 cup King Street Stout
1 cup packed brown sugar
1 teaspoon vanilla paste
    (available at specialty
    stores and online)
1 cup macadamia nuts,
    roughly chopped
½ cup dark chocolate chunks

This recipe ties together the King Street Stout, dark chocolate, brown sugar and macadamia nuts for a rich and rewarding ice cream. The vanilla bean paste called for is actually a heavy syrup which contains the vanilla beans normally scraped from whole pods. The result is a fragrant, speckled product with real vanilla bean flavor.

....

Mix cream, beer, brown sugar and vanilla paste in a bowl until sugar is dissolved.

Pour mixture into an ice cream maker and follow manufacturer's instructions.

Fold macadamia nuts and dark chocolate into ice cream mixture. Cover and freeze for at least 4 hours.

WIT CREME BRULEE

Michael Bump, *Restaurant Orsay*

YIELDS FIVE 7-OUNCE PORTIONS

1 ½ cups heavy cream
1 cup Belgian Wit Bier
Zest of ½ lemon
10 cloves
12 egg yolks from large eggs
1 cup sugar, plus more for
    bruleeing tops of custards
Granulated white sugar

A light brew in the form of Belgian Wit goes into this impressive brulee. The crisp, coriander flavor goes deliciously with the lemon and clove in the rich custard.

Preheat oven to 300°F.

Put cream, beer, zest and cloves in a pot and heat to a simmer.

In a separate bowl mix together the egg yolks and 1 cup sugar. Slowly pour the hot cream and beer mixture into the egg mixture, whisking constantly. Strain the mixture to remove the zest, cloves and any cooked egg.

Place five ramekins on a shallow flat pan in the oven. (Note: Shallow ramekins are recommended in this recipe. The custard will cook more evenly and yield a better finished product.)

Carefully pour the custard mixture into the ramekins, filling them about a 1/4 inch from the top. Fill the pan up with water to come halfway up the sides of the ramekins. Close the oven door and bake for approximately an hour to an hour and a half. The custards will be slightly jiggly in the center.

Remove ramekins carefully from water bath and allow to cool in refrigerator for at least 4 hours.

When custards are completely cool, use a paper towel to gently dab away any moisture or condensation that has formed on the tops of the custards. Be careful not to dent the custard.

Sprinkle the tops of the custards with granulated white sugar. Be generous and make sure to cover the whole surface. Swirl the ramekins to distribute the sugar evenly and pour off any excess.

Turn on your torch and slow move it around on the sugar, keeping the torch a couple inches from the custards.

Keep the flame moving so it isn't focused on any one spot for too long. After a few seconds the sugar will start to darken and form a glass-like crust. Once tops are golden place crème brulees back in the refrigerator for a minute or two to harden.

I-10 PLUM HOPSICLES

Tommy Davis, *The Hyppo*

MAKES AROUND 25 POPS (DEPENDING ON THE SIZE OF THE MOLD YOU'RE USING)

3 ½ **quarts plums, halved, seeds removed**
2 – 12 **ounce cans I-10 IPA**
3 **cups raw cane sugar**
½ **teaspoon sea salt**

There's nothing like a popsicle to cool you down on a hot day. Here on the First Coast, that's all but those two weeks in January when you turn the air conditioner off. This gorgeously plummy offering from Tommy Davis at The Hyppo in St. Augustine will chill you out with an added super hoppy hit of I-10 IPA. Whew!

Add all ingredients to a blender and blend until well mixed. Pour mixture into popsicle molds and place in freezer until frozen.

ACKNOWLEDGEMENTS

Cari Sánchez-Potter

Cari Sanchez-Potter is the General Manager of Intuition Ale Works. She has been with the brewery since it opened in 2010 and oversees all marketing, communications, community relations and event planning initiatives.

Cari is also Owner and Executive Producer of The Legend Series, a quarterly pop-up art and dining series that showcases the best of Northeast Florida's culinary, visual and performing arts in highly unusual locations.

Her personal mission is to foster a vibrant food, drink and arts culture in Northeast Florida. She has contributed food articles to a number of local and national publications, is a co-founder of a local farmers market and is a sought-after food judge.

Cari holds a BS in Marketing from Boston College and an MA in Gastronomy from The University of Adelaide / Le Cordon Bleu in South Australia. Her experience living on five different continents has informed her approach to the local cultural and culinary initiatives she spearheads.

Robin Rütenberg

Robin Rütenberg is the Creative Projects Coordinator at Intuition Ale Works. She assists Intuition in social media outreach, planning events and unique undertakings, leading tours and tastings at the brewery and serving as a representative at off-site events. She is devoted to the philosophy behind quality craft beer and is passionate about cultivating the community of Jacksonville craft breweries and their supporters.

Robin earned BBAs in Economics and in International Business from the University of North Florida in 2010 and became a Certified Cicerone Beer Server in early 2012.

When not at the brewery, Robin is exploring sounds and songwriting. She performs regionally with her bands Four Families and The Little Books. She is also a founding board member of Girls Rock Jacksonville, a non-profit music empowerment camp for girls.

Laura Evans

After attending Parsons in NYC, getting a BFA in Communication and Design from UNF and working in advertising for big corporate clients, Laura Evans opened her photo studio and said, "I really don't want to take portraits. Or photograph food." True story from which she's learned the best road to travel is the least-expected, most-challenging one - as long as it has craft breweries and vegetarian food along the way. Her current goals are to qualify for the Boston Marathon, work on a David Lynch film and take a self-portrait that is in focus.

Jodi Kasten

Jodi Kasten is a writer and copy editor who stubbornly remains in Arlington because the parking situation is magnificent. She was raised in Gulf Breeze, Florida and educated at the University of Central Arkansas. She is the genius who invented the Mug Club tag system and the sassy introductions for most of the recipes in this book. When she's not fixing words, she creates jams and sausages with her husband and four children. She describes her career as "that place behind the curtain where the levers are pulled."

Staci Bu Shea

Staci is an independent curator and writer based in Jacksonville, Florida. She graduated with a BA in Art History from the University of North Florida and Sophia University with a concentration in Japanese and Chinese Art History. She is a Curatorial Assistant to artist Jim Draper and works collaboratively with artists who primarily work with site-specificity, social practice and the internet to forge thoughtful and thematic exhibitions. It is late in the night that she finds herself working on graphic design, specifically for exhibition-related media, catalogues, artists' books, zines, one-off programs for The Legend Series and creative projects for Intuition Ale Works. Staci loves all things printed and hopes that you'll find this book to be a beautiful, informative object. She joined Intuition in early 2012 to get close to the craft and is currently studying for her Cicerone Beer Server certification. As an artist, she appreciates the fun and creative opportunities that Intuition has offered her.

RESTAURANT INDEX